THE OFFICIAL COOKBOOK

Seinfeld™

THE OFFICIAL COOKBOOK

Recipes by Julie Tremaine
Written by Brendan Kirby

Photography by Emily Hawkes

INSIGHT
EDITIONS

San Rafael · Los Angeles · London

CONTENTS

INTRODUCTION

What are you in the mood to eat tonight? Nothing? Perfect. "Let's cut the bull, sister!" because you've found the right book, and no library cop will come after you for it. We hope. As our favorite show has taught us so memorably, even nothing is something; and this even extends to food.

Throughout *Seinfeld's* legendary original nine-year run, casual fans and rabid aficionados alike had a front row seat to the adventures of the Fabulous Foursome as they encountered every social situation imaginable in their own unique and hilarious way. Along the journey, however, they needed to eat. Oh, and eat they did, Jerry. They were out there and they were loving every minute of it; whether at Monk's, 129 W 81st Street, George Steinbrenner's office, Mendy's, or even, um, Reggie's (that's right, "Reggie's, Jerry! REGGIE's!"), the gang always made time for their sustenance. While they noshed, we observed with a keen eye and are now ready to share a portion of what we found. However, this is no instructional video on how to make your own sausages. Inspired by plot lines, characters, memorable themes, dialogue, and beyond, here is your chance to toss on an apron as you prepare *Seinfeld*-inspired meals, desserts, and more that will, as George would say, "illuminate the mind and dazzle the eye."

Are you ready to be master of the *Seinfeld* culinary domain? Or will you be left out and ostracized like the Bubble Boy? There's only one way to find out: Giddyap and let's start the insanity! We hope you enjoy and have some fun with these culinary comedy classics.

MEET THE CAST

JERRY

Jerome Seinfeld of 129 W. 81st St (Apt. 5A) is the link between this unparalleled fantastic foursome. Childhood friend of George, neighbor and confidant of Kramer, Elaine's ex, he knows all of their idiosyncrasies and has a front row seat to all of their misadventures. In between stand-up sets and making, in the words of Newman, "inane observations" we like to think Jerry would attempt to prepare all of the dishes in this book. However, in HIS own words: *"I tell ya, I don't see it happening!"* That's a shame . . .

KRAMER

He's Cosmo Kramer and what really can we say? No one lives a life like Kramer, and Jerry does his part to enable that lifestyle by letting the K-Man draft off his wake of food, fame, and, sometimes, women! Mr. Kramer possesses quite the entrepreneurial spirit as well, and as founder of Kramerica Industries, we like to think he'd say "Giddyup" to the idea of this book.

GEORGE

George Louis Costanza has many "alleged" talents and skills: Expert in Risk Management, Architecture, slipping Mickeys, and of course, lying. He's also written a sitcom pilot, claimed to have written a play, and been caught by his mother enjoying a touch of self-gratification. He's disturbed, he's depressed, he's inadequate. He's got it all!

ELAINE

Elaine Marie Benes might be the most professional and admirable character—although that might not be saying much. She has held down several successful jobs, maintained an active social life, can tell you where you can clean up if you need extra Today sponges, and so much more. Just keep her away from Poppy Seed Bagels and do not put her in charge of running the J. Peterman Company.

NEWMAN

Jerry's nemesis warned us all that "when you control the mail, you control INFORMATION!" Though he's evil, diabolical, portly (yes), he's also, in the words of George "merry" and admittedly, "extremely regimented about his meals." Certainly, he'd squeeze in a few selections of this book in between mail deliveries.

SOUP NAZI

Eccentric would be a decent start when attempting to label this genius of the Upper West Side. He is regimented, disciplined, and knows exactly what he demands from his customers. Why should he expect anything less? Perhaps we could all learn something from his stern rules. Can't follow them? Put this book back on your shelf and come back in ONE YEAR! Or maybe just one minute, it's fine, it's our book and we won't tell him . . .

No soup for you!

J. PETERMAN

What do we truly know about the charismatic and enigmatic owner of the J. Peterman Sales Company? Well for starters he puts Elaine in charge of running it so perhaps that tells us all we need to know. Despite a decision that resulted in the Urban Sombrero ("the horror!"), you can't hold everything against him. Truly a man of simple pleasures, as evidenced by his sparse apartment, his inclusion in this book would certainly cause he and Mother to swell with pride, and maybe even celebrate with a last-minute return excursion to Burma?

DAVID PUDDY

From his obsession with Arby's to assisting Kramer in installing a garbage disposal in his bathtub, Puddy has dabbled peripherally around different food-related scenarios. Would any of his favorite dishes cause him to paint his face in support of his preferred foods? Or maybe that's just saved for hockey playoff games? Either way, squint and stare your way through these recipes to complete your David Puddy—inspired experience.

JUSTIN PITT

A man on the hunt for the perfect pair of socks, a salt-less pretzel, and the opportunity to hold a rope for the Woody Woodpecker balloon in the Thanksgiving Day parade would undoubtedly work up an appetite and need his share of sustenance. One of Mr. Pitt's legendary idiosyncrasies figures heavily into the pantheon of great *Seinfeld* moments. We'll supply the recipe, you need your own knife, fork, and Snickers bars.

TIMMY

I mean, really? Does a one-episode, one-scene character deserve a place of honor with a bio alongside such *Seinfeld*ian royalty? GET OUT! HOWEVER, his sole contribution resulted in "double-dipping" entering the pop culture vernacular and thus, forever cementing him within *Seinfeld* lore. Don't appreciate his inclusion here? No problem. Just take one look at this blurb and END IT!

GEORGE COSTANZA

FAMILY
Frank/Estelle Costanza
Cousin Shelly
Brother (Unnamed)
Aunt Baby

ACQUAINTANCES
Beena

JERRY SEINFELD

FAMILY
Morty/Helen Seinfeld
Sister
Uncle Leo
Nana
Cousin Jeffrey
Aunt Stella
Aunt Silvia
Cousin Artie Levine
Cousin Douglas

ACQUAINTANCES
Kenny Bania
Alec Berg
Babu Bhatt
The Doorman
Milosh
Joel Horneck
Phil Tatola
Ramon
Fulton

ACQUAINTANCES
Al Netche
Gary Fogel
Joe Davola

ACQUAINTANCES
Mickey Abbot
Mike Moffit
Bob Cobb (The Maestro)
Sally Weaver
Jimmy

CLOSEST FRIEND
Elaine Benes

ACQUAINTANCES
Phil (neighbor)

CLOSEST FRIEND
Cosmo Kramer

ACQUAINTANCES
Joe Mayo

ACQUAINTANCES
Newman
The Drake
Tim Whatley

CLOSEST FRIE
Jerry Seinfeld

CLOSEST FRIEND
George Costanza

ACQUAINTANCES
Poppie

FAMILY
Babs Kramer

ACQUAINTANCES
Tor Eckman
Stan the Caddy
Darin the Intern
Jackie Chiles
Slippery Pete/Schlomo
Franklin Delano Romanowski
Corky Rameriz/Lomez/Bob
Sacamano/Jay Reimenschneider

COSMO KRAMER

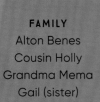

ELAINE BENES

FAMILY
Alton Benes
Cousin Holly
Grandma Mema
Gail (sister)

ACQUAINTANCES
Tina Robbins
Jean-Paul
Sue Ellen Mischke
Winona
Rabbi Glickman
Wendy
Gene/Feldman/Kevin

CHAPTER 1

BREAKFAST

"More cereal?" —Jerry
"THE INVITATIONS," SEASON 7

Even though Jerry can break up with a woman for ANY reason, he'll never break up with cereal. Whatever your plan for the day ahead may be, whether hitting golf balls into the ocean or slipping the boss a Mickey, you can't do it on an empty stomach. Start the day of deplorable behavior off right with a solid *Seinfeld*-style breakfast.

~~MR. LIPPMAN'S~~ ELAINE'S MUFFIN TOPS

PREP TIME: 15 MINUTES • COOK TIME: 11 MINUTES • YIELD: 40 MINI MUFFIN TOPS

"Pop the top, toss the stump!" says Elaine, because, well, this was her idea. Contrary to Mr. Lippman's view, these concepts aren't "all in the air!" They do, in fact, come out of someone's air, in this case Elaine Marie Benes'—so salute the queen with a batch. As for the leftover stumps, you're on your own. Don't assume everyone will want them, or risk an irate Rebecca De Mornay hunting you down.

2 cups all-purpose flour

1 teaspoon baking powder

1 teaspoon baking soda

1 teaspoon salt

½ cup (1 stick) unsalted butter, softened

¼ cup granulated sugar

¼ brown sugar

2 teaspoons vanilla extract

½ cup honey

1 teaspoon cinnamon

2 large eggs

½ cup milk

12 ounces of fresh or frozen (not thawed) blueberries

Preheat the oven to 400°F.

In a medium bowl, combine the flour, baking powder, baking soda, and salt. Set aside.

In the bowl of a mixer fitted with a flat beater, add the butter, granulated sugar, and brown sugar. Mix on medium for 2 minutes, then add the vanilla, honey, and cinnamon and mix 1 minute more. Add the eggs and mix for another minute. Be sure to scrape down the sides of the bowl frequently.

Add half the dry ingredients, then the milk, then the remaining dry ingredients. Scrape down the bowl between additions.

Remove the bowl from mixer and fold in the blueberries.

Prepare a mini muffin top pan by spraying it with nonstick cooking spray.

Spoon ½ tablespoon of batter into each muffin top indentation. Clean any overflow between the indentations to prevent muffins from baking together.

Bake for about 9 to 11 minutes until lightly golden.

JERRY'S CEREAL BARS

PREP TIME: 5 MINUTES • COOK TIME: 5 MINUTES PLUS 1 HOUR CHILLING TIME • YIELD: 12 BARS

"She even orders cereal at a restaurant!" exclaims Jerry, as his then-girlfriend Jeannie Steinman ("J.S.!") taps directly into his, as Kramer calls it, "Peter Pan complex." Taking Jerry's love of cereal, but removing the milk-soaked aspect, gives us these bars with everything we need to kick off the day. Take some for on-the-go needs as well. Whether running late to a meeting with Mr. Wilhelm or heading to your parents' house in Queens, these bars will hit the spot.

4 cups dry cereal of your choice

½ cup sliced almonds, or other nuts

½ dried cranberries, or other fruit

½ cup mini marshmallows

¾ cup creamy peanut butter, or almond butter

½ cup honey

½ teaspoon vanilla extract

Line an 11-by-7-inch baking pan with parchment paper.

In a large mixing bowl, combine the cereal, almonds, cranberries, and mini marshmallows.

In a small saucepan, melt the peanut butter, honey, and vanilla over medium heat until totally melted, about 3 to 5 minutes.

Pour the mixture over the dry ingredients and stir until evenly distributed. Transfer to the baking pan and cover with another sheet of parchment paper. Press down firmly to flatten to a uniform level.

Chill for at least 1 hour. Remove the top parchment paper and slice into bars, then serve.

NEWMAN'S COFFEE CAKE

PREP TIME: 10 MINUTES • COOK TIME: 34 MINUTES • YIELD: 8 TO 10 SERVINGS

"A whole BOX OF THEM!" is the amount you'll want to whip up. This coffee cake is so good that friends will promise anything in exchange for one, just like Newman did with Jerry. You'll even think of everyone's favorite antagonistic letter carrier while savoring every bite of this "crumby" classic. Eat it for breakfast right away or store a few pieces in your mail bag if you're "saving it for later." You'll respect this breakfast treat the same way Jerry "respects a good coma."

FOR THE CAKE
6 tablespoons unsalted butter, softened

½ cup granulated sugar

2 eggs

1½ teaspoons vanilla extract

⅓ cup buttermilk

1¼ cups cake flour

½ teaspoon baking soda

¼ teaspoon salt

FOR THE CRUMB TOPPING
½ cup granulated sugar

½ cup dark brown sugar

1 teaspoon cinnamon

½ teaspoon salt

1½ cups cake flour

½ cup (1 stick) unsalted butter, melted

TO MAKE THE CAKE:
Preheat the oven to 325°F.

Spray parchment paper with nonstick cooking spray and use to line an 8-inch round cake pan.

In the bowl of a mixer fitted with a flat beater, beat the butter and sugar for 1 minute. When completely incorporated, add the eggs, vanilla, and buttermilk and continue beating the mixture.

In a medium mixing bowl, whisk together the flour, baking soda, and salt. While the mixer is running, slowly add the dry ingredients into the mixing bowl. Make sure all ingredients are completely incorporated and the batter is smooth.

Pour batter into the prepared cake pan.

TO MAKE THE CRUMB TOPPING:
In the bowl of a mixer fitted with a flat beater, combine the granulated sugar, brown sugar, cinnamon, salt, and flour. Mix on low. Beat in the melted butter a little at a time. Do not over beat; there should be lumps of various sizes and some ingredients should still be dry.

Sprinkle the crumble evenly on top of the prepared cake batter. Do not mix it into the batter; it should sit on top.

Bake for about 32 to 34 minutes. Test doneness of the cake by inserting a knife into the center and taking it out quickly. If there is wet batter on the knife, it needs a few more minutes of baking time. If it comes out clean, the cake is done.

Let the cake cool in the pan for 20 minutes, then remove the cake from the pan by lifting out the parchment paper. Let the cake cool completely before transfering to a serving dish.

FORBIDDEN BAGELS

PREP TIME: 60 MINUTES PLUS OVERNIGHT RISING TIME • COOK TIME: 25 MINUTES • YIELD: 8 BAGELS

Beware of savory poppy seeds if a work-ordered drug test is looming; a fate worse than Elaine's may await any unfortunate soul who eats too many of these sumptuous dough rings. But now for the real test: Can you prep a batch as solidly as the crew at H&H Bagels? Give them a try. We won't tell Mr. Peterman.

FOR THE YEAST MIXTURE
1½ teaspoons active dry yeast
3 teaspoons granulated sugar
⅓ cup warm water

FOR THE BAGELS
4 cups bread flour
2½ teaspoons salt
1 tablespoon vegetable oil
⅔ cup warm water
1 tablespoon brown sugar
¼ cup poppy seeds

TO MAKE THE YEAST MIXTURE:
In a small mixing bowl, combine the yeast, granulated sugar, and warm water. Let sit for 5 minutes.

TO MAKE THE BAGELS:
In the bowl of a mixer fitted with a dough hook, combine the yeast mixture, flour, salt, and oil. With the mixer on low, slowly add ⅔ cup warm water. Turn off the mixer and scrape down the sides of the bowl. When you can no longer see any dry ingredients, continue to knead the dough in the mixer for another 7 minutes.

Test the dough by pulling off a golf ball–size piece and stretching it out very thin. The dough should be transparent; if it is not, knead it for another 2 to 3 minutes.

Let the dough rest on a large flat surface for 15 minutes. Using your hands, separate dough into 8 equal sized balls and let them rest for an additional 15 minutes.

Holding a ball with both hands, use your thumbs to create a 2-inch hole in the center. Place the bagels on a baking sheet lined with parchment paper and spray the dough with nonstick cooking spray. Loosely cover bagels with plastic wrap and refrigerate overnight.

When ready to bake the bagels, preheat the oven to 450°F.

In a large saucepan over high heat, bring a pot of water to boil. Add the brown sugar and stir to dissolve. Place 2 or 3 bagels in boiling water, leaving enough room so the bagels don't touch. Boil on each side for 45 seconds. Remove bagels from water, drain, and return to the sheet pan. Repeat with the remaining bagels. Sprinkle with poppy seeds.

Bake for 15 to 18 minutes until golden brown. Remove from the oven and cool slightly before serving.

"CERTAIN TIME" CANTALOUPE BREAKFAST BOWL

PREP TIME: 10 MINUTES • YIELD: 2 SERVINGS

The idiosyncrasies of the Fab Four are head-scratching and prevalent throughout the duration of the series. And though Jerry may admit to only eating cantaloupe as he sees fit, or at "certain times," his own persnicketiness does not have to dictate anyone else's choices. Like the *Seinfeld* dialogue, this bowl is snappy, fresh, and timeless.

1 cantaloupe

2 cups plain Greek yogurt, divided

½ cup granola, divided

½ cup blueberries, or raspberries, divided

¼ cup sliced almonds, or pepitas, divided

4 teaspoons maple syrup, divided (optional)

Prepare the cantaloupe "bowls" by cutting the melon in half using a sharp kitchen knife. Discard the pulp.

Divide the yogurt evenly between the two melon halves, then top each with half the granola and half the berries.

Top each bowl with half the almonds or pepitas.

For a sweeter breakfast bowl, drizzle 2 teaspoons maple syrup on each one—though if your fruit is fully ripe, you may not need it.

KRAMER'S PEACH PANCAKES

PREP TIME: 20 MINUTES • COOK TIME: 25 MINUTES • YIELD: 8 TO 10 PANCAKES

"The Mackinaw Peaches, Jerry! The Mackinaw Peaches!" Though these elusive delights might be Cosmo's peach of choice, any variety will do for this breakfast, which can be prepared more often than just two weeks out of the year. Who knows? Maybe the health benefits of the peaches will have you "ripe" enough to pose for Calvin Klein, just like the K-Man.

FOR THE PEACH COMPOTE

4 medium fresh peaches, or 1 pound frozen peaches

¼ cup maple syrup

1 teaspoon cinnamon

2 tablespoons orange juice

¼ cup water

FOR THE PANCAKES

1 cup all-purpose flour

2 teaspoons baking powder

½ teaspoon salt

2 tablespoons granulated sugar

1 cup milk

1 egg, beaten

2 tablespoons unsalted butter, melted

1 teaspoon vanilla extract

TO MAKE THE PEACH COMPOTE:

Chop the peaches, discarding the pits. Peel first if desired, but it's not totally necessary. In a medium saucepan over medium-high heat, combine the peaches, maple syrup, orange juice, and water. Bring to a boil, then reduce heat and simmer for about 10 minutes, until the fruit has softened and the sauce has thickened. If the compote is very thick, add more water to achieve your ideal consistency. Remove from heat and set aside.

TO MAKE THE PANCAKES:

In a mixing bowl, combine the flour, baking powder, salt, and sugar. Add milk, egg, butter, and vanilla. Mix well and let sit for 10 minutes.

Spray a large skillet with nonstick cooking spray, then heat over medium flame. Drop the batter by the spoonful into the pan, being careful not to crowd the pancakes.

Cook until golden brown and air bubbles have risen to the surface, about 3 minutes. Flip and cook another 2 to 3 minutes until golden brown. Remove from the heat, transfer to a plate, and tent with aluminum foil to keep the pancakes warm.

Repeat with the rest of the batter. Serve with the peach compote.

CHAPTER 2

NO DOUBLE-DIPPING

"Just take one dip and end it!" —Timmy

"THE IMPLANT," SEASON 4

Double-dipping is "like putting your whole mouth right in the dip!" As much as we love George, Timmy makes a valid point. Despite their ugly and unfortunate interaction, that hilarious scene has helped us to compile an "admittedly rudimentary" list of crowd-pleasing dips and a salsa, because, yes, "people like to say SALSA!" These will take late-night grazing to the next level, delight party guests, and so much more. One word of advice: If you do have a gathering, don't invite Timmy AND George.

HUMMUS AMONG US

PREP TIME: 5 MINUTES PLUS 1 HOUR CHILLING TIME • YIELD: 2 CUPS

"Because you thought your breath smelled like hummus. . . ." When George is dating a lady-Jerry, Janet, we learn about his preference for gum after he's told that his breath has the less-than-envious smell of chickpeas and garlic. And since there's nothing wrong with fresh breath, we recommend giving in to that hankering for a stick of double-mint freshness after consuming this one.

One 14.5-ounce can chickpeas, drained

¼ cup tahini paste

1 clove garlic

Juice of 1 lemon

½ teaspoon salt

3 tablespoons olive oil

2 tablespoons cold water (optional)

In the bowl of a food processor, combine the chickpeas, tahini, garlic, lemon juice, and salt. Mix for 2 minutes.

While the processor is running, slowly pour in the olive oil. Mix for 2 more minutes. For a creamier texture, add in 2 tablespoons of cold water and mix for 1 more minute.

Remove to a bowl, then cover and refrigerate for at least 1 hour.

MÉNAGE À DIPS

A ménage à dips? "Are you "INTO IT?!" Maybe one of these selections was the one Timmy and George fought over. Who knows? If the situation calls for double-dipping, do so with discretion. Though Timmy would disapprove, George has got your back. Whatever the pleasure, these classics will satisfy.

ONION DIP

PREP TIME: 10 MINUTES
COOK TIME: 15 MINUTES PLUS 1 HOUR OR
OVERNIGHT CHILLING TIME
YIELD: 8 TO 10 SERVINGS

2 tablespoons unsalted butter

2 medium yellow onions, minced

4 garlic cloves, minced

2 teaspoons onion powder

1 teaspoon garlic salt

1 teaspoon salt

2 cups sour cream

1 tablespoon fresh chives, chopped

In a medium skillet over medium heat, melt the butter. Add the onions and cook about 15 minutes until golden brown, taking care not to burn them.

Add the garlic and cook for 1 more minute. Remove from heat and transfer to a bowl.

Fold in spices and allow to cool.

Fold in sour cream and chill for at least 1 hour or overnight.

Garnish with chives before serving.

BAKED QUESO DIP

PREP TIME: 5 MINUTES
COOK TIME: 25 MINUTES
YIELD: 6 SERVINGS

½ small yellow onion, minced

2 cloves garlic, minced

One 4-ounce can green chiles

1 pound Oaxaca, or mozzarella cheese, grated

Preheat the oven to 400°F.

In a medium skillet, cook the onion and garlic over medium-high heat until golden brown, about 5 minutes. Add the chiles and stir to combine.

Spray an 8-by-10-inch baking dish with nonstick cooking spray, then pour in the mixture.

Add cheese and bake until the mixture is browned and bubbling, about 20 minutes. Serve hot, with warm tortillas or tortilla chips.

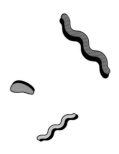

HOT SPINACH ARTICHOKE DIP

PREP TIME: 10 MINUTES
COOK TIME: 10 MINUTES
YIELD: 10 SERVINGS

1 sourdough boule

2 tablespoons unsalted butter

4 garlic cloves, minced

One 15-ounce can artichoke hearts,
  drained and chopped

10 ounces fresh or frozen spinach,
  well-drained and chopped

1 teaspoon salt

8 ounces cream cheese

½ cup mayonnaise

½ cup sour cream

1 cup shredded mozzarella

1 cup grated Parmesan

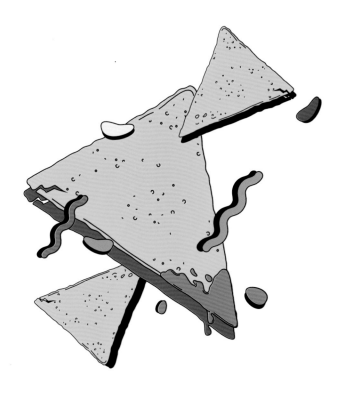

Prepare the bread bowl by cutting a large circle in the center of the boule and removing the bread. Hollow out most of the insides, taking care to leave ½ inch of bread near the crust and not to pierce the crust.

Cut the bread you've removed into bite-size chunks. Place the bread bowl on a serving platter and arrange the bread chunks around it.

Melt the butter in a large skillet over medium heat. Add the garlic and cook for 2 minutes until fragrant and starting to brown. Add the artichoke hearts, spinach, and salt and sauté until the spinach is wilted, about 3 minutes.

Lower heat to medium-low and fold in the cream cheese, mayonnaise, and sour cream, stirring until combined. Add the mozzarella and Parmesan and cook, stirring constantly, until the cheese is melted and the dip is hot.

Remove from heat and transfer the dip to the bread bowl. Serve hot.

#1 SALSA IN AMERICA

PREP TIME: 10 MINUTES • YIELD: 3 TO 4 CUPS

I said "SELTZER!" not "SALSA!" Although you can pair this salsa with a seltzer and do a salsa dance when you're done making it, the Urban Sombrero is not included with this recipe. As in the case of Morty Seinfeld's #1 Dad T-shirt, we're not sure "how official any of these rankings really are," but it's our recipe so for "*Seinfeld*ian" purposes, this is number one.

½ white onion, roughly chopped

1 clove garlic, chopped

1 to 2 jalapeños, seeded and chopped

One 4-ounce can diced green chiles, drained

2 firm Roma tomatoes, chopped

One 14.5-ounce can chopped roasted tomatoes

¼ teaspoon salt

¼ teaspoon ground cumin

½ cup roughly chopped fresh cilantro

In the bowl of a food processor, combine the onion and garlic and process until finely minced. Add 1 jalapeño and 1 tablespoon of green chiles for medium-spicy salsa or add more or less depending on your preference. Process for 30 seconds, then add the Roma tomatoes and briefly pulse the mixture.

Drain the roasted tomatoes of about half their liquid, then add them along with the remaining liquid into the bowl of the processor. Add the salt, cumin, and cilantro. Process for 30 seconds to 1 minute, depending on how chunky you prefer your salsa.

MRS. CHOATE'S MARBLE RYE

PREP TIME: 45 MINUTES PLUS 2 HOURS RISING TIME • COOK TIME: 40 MINUTES • YIELD: 1 LOAF

With apologies to Mrs. Choate—after all, Jerry DID steal her marble rye—what else would we dip into one of our recommended concoctions? We hope some marble rye bread will hit the spot. Pieces can even be fastened to a fishing line to assist with dipping. Just make sure your fiancée and future in-laws aren't home while you do that. It could be awkward.

FOR THE LIGHT RYE

1 cup warm water

1½ teaspoons active dry yeast

1½ teaspoons kosher salt

1 tablespoon molasses

1 tablespoon neutral cooking oil plus more for rising bowl

1½ cups all-purpose flour

1½ cups rye flour

FOR THE DARK RYE

1 cup warm water

1½ teaspoons active dry yeast

1½ teaspoons kosher salt

1 tablespoon molasses

1 tablespoon neutral cooking oil plus more for rising bowl

1½ cups all-purpose flour

1½ cups rye flour

2 tablespoons dark cocoa powder

TO MAKE THE LIGHT RYE:

In the bowl of a mixer, combine the water and yeast and let sit about 5 minutes. Add the salt and molasses and mix to combine. Put the bowl on the mixer fitted with a dough hook and add the oil, all-purpose flour, and rye flour.

Knead on medium speed, being sure that all ingredients are incorporated. You may need to stop the mixer and turn the dough over by hand to ensure all ingredients are mixed in. The dough should be tacky, not wet. If it is too wet, add 1 tablespoon of flour; if too dry, add 1 tablespoon of water.

Continue kneading on medium for about 7 minutes. Dough should bounce back when poked.

Oil a large bowl and place the dough into it. Be sure that the dough is evenly coated with oil. Loosely cover bowl with plastic wrap and let dough rise for 1 hour.

TO MAKE THE DARK RYE:

Again, combine the water and yeast in the bowl of the mixer, and let it sit about 5 minutes. Add the salt and molasses and mix to combine. Fit the mixer with the dough hook and add oil, all-purpose flour, rye flour, and cocoa powder.

Repeat the steps to knead, oil, and let the dough rise.

Recipe continues on next page . . .

TO MAKE THE MARBLE RYE:

Preheat the oven to 450°F.

Line a baking sheet with parchment paper.

Punch down each ball of dough to release the air. Roll out the lighter dough to a 12-by-18-inch rectangle. Roll out the darker dough to the same size.

Place the darker dough on top of the lighter dough, then using the heels of your hands, push down on the two doughs to make them stick together.

Roll the combined dough tightly, starting at the short end of the rectangle. Crimp the ends and roll the dough back and forth so the loaf will stick together.

Place the rolled loaf seam side down on the baking sheet. Loosely cover the dough with plastic wrap and let rise for 1 hour until doubled in size.

Cut ½-inch diagonal scores into the top of the loaf.

Place the loaf in the oven and immediately turn the oven temperature down to 350°F.

Bake approximately 40 minutes until golden brown. Let cool completely on the baking sheet before serving.

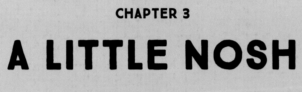

CHAPTER 3

A LITTLE NOSH

"So, anything to, uh, nosh?" —George
"THE COUCH," SEASON 6

When George wants "real movie atmosphere" at home, he turns down the lights and gets himself an appropriate snack. And while these small bites may be ideal enhancements for almost any activity, we recommend pairing them with a great film. Ideally, we'd go with *Breakfast at Tiffany's*, but any movie could work. We'll get you started with a few suggestions: Take one with you to *The Other Side of Darkness* or pack one in your *Sack Lunch* while venturing through the *Chunnel* as you make "a strange, erotic journey from Milan to Minsk."

PUFFY SHIRT PASTRY TARTS

PREP TIME: 15 MINUTES • COOK TIME: 25 MINUTES • YIELD: 6 SERVINGS

"I agreed to wear this?!" Don't worry, there's no need to slip into one of these for a big TV interview. The pirate look may have been the new look for the '90s, but maybe these tarts will be the snack for the new millennium. Watch out for heckling if you make these, however: "Avast ye pastry?" What does that even mean?!

6 frozen puff pastry shells

3 tablespoons unsalted butter

1 large leek, tender white and green parts only, thinly sliced

8 ounces baby bella mushrooms, thinly sliced

¼ teaspoon salt

¼ teaspoon pepper

1 tablespoon fresh rosemary, chopped

1 teaspoon fresh thyme, chopped

¾ cup grated Asiago cheese, or Pecorino Romano cheese, divided

¼ cup Fontina cheese

Preheat the oven to 400°F.

Line a sheet pan with parchment paper. Place the frozen pastry shells on the pan and bake according to package directions. When fully baked, transfer pastry shells to a wire rack and allow to cool, then gently hollow out the centers of the pastries.

In a large skillet over medium heat, melt the butter. Add leeks and cook until softened, about 3 minutes. Add mushrooms, salt, and pepper. Cook for about 5 to 6 minutes, until mushrooms are softened and reduced in size. Add rosemary and thyme and cook for 1 more minute.

Transfer the mixture to a bowl and fold in ½ cup of the Asiago or Pecorino Romano cheese and the Fontina.

Place the puff pastry shells on a baking sheet and divide the leek-mushroom-cheese mixture evenly between them. Top with the remaining cheese.

Bake until the cheese on top is melted, about 5 minutes. Serve hot.

GEORGE'S JERK STORE SHRIMP

PREP TIME: 10 MINUTES PLUS 1 HOUR CHILLING TIME • COOK TIME: 5 MINUTES • YIELD: 1 CUP

"Hey George, the ocean called . . . they're running out of shrimp"! A classic app or snack, just don't order a platter for the conference room table. Enjoy from the comfort of home—or at the Jerk Store— and see how many can fit in your mouth at once. Flying to Akron, meeting with Riley, and telling him you had sex with his wife is optional.

FOR THE COCKTAIL SAUCE

1 cup ketchup

2 teaspoons lemon juice

1½ tablespoons prepared horseradish

½ teaspoon Worcestershire sauce

1 pound large raw shrimp, peeled and deveined

TO MAKE THE COCKTAIL SAUCE:

In a medium glass bowl, combine the ketchup, lemon juice, horseradish, and Worcestershire sauce. Adjust spices to taste and chill for at least 1 hour.

TO PREPARE THE SHRIMP:

Fill a medium saucepan halfway with water and bring to a boil over high heat. Add the shrimp and cook until opaque, about 3 minutes.

Drain shrimp and remove immediately to a bowl of ice water to stop the cooking process. Let sit for 1 minute, then drain and chill until ready to serve. Serve with cocktail sauce.

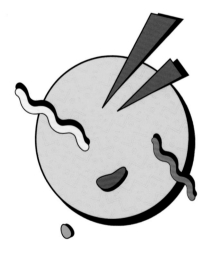

KRAMER'S PETERMAN REALITY TOUR PIZZA BAGELS

PREP TIME: 25 MINUTES PLUS 30 MINUTES RISING TIME AND OVERNIGHT CHILLING TIME
COOK TIME: 24 MINUTES • YIELD: 32 PIECES

These probably won't run to $37.50, and there's no rule that says you have to be on any kind of Kramer-inspired "Reality Bus Tour" to enjoy them. Complete the experience by closing your eyes and pretending to be driving past Lomez's place of worship while enjoying these little numbers. As for Kramer, just don't forget that, "The last thing this guy is qualified to give a tour of is reality."

FOR THE BAGELS
1½ teaspoons active dry yeast

3 teaspoons granulated sugar

1 cup warm water, divided

4 cups bread flour

2½ teaspoon salt

1 tablespoon vegetable oil

FOR THE PIZZA BAGELS
2 cups tomato sauce

2 teaspoons dried oregano

1 teaspoon kosher salt

1 teaspoon pepper

2 teaspoons red pepper flakes (optional)

4 cups shredded mozzarella

TO MAKE THE BAGELS:

In a small mixing bowl, combine the yeast, granulated sugar, and ⅓ cup water. Let sit for 5 minutes.

In the bowl of a mixer fitted with a dough hook, combine the yeast mixture, flour, salt, and oil. With the mixer on low, slowly add the remaining ⅔ cup water. Turn off the mixer and scrape down the sides of the bowl. When you can no longer see any dry ingredients, continue to knead another 7 minutes.

Test the dough by pulling off a golf ball–size piece and stretching it out very thin. The dough should be transparent. If it is not, knead for another 2 to 3 minutes.

Line a sheet pan with parchment paper.

Place dough on a large flat surface and let it rest for 15 minutes. Using your hands, separate dough into 16 equal-size balls and let them rest for an additional 15 minutes.

Holding a dough ball with two hands, use your thumbs to create a 1-inch hole in the center. Place the bagels on the sheet pan and spray them with nonstick cooking spray. Loosely cover bagels with plastic wrap and refrigerate overnight.

When ready to bake the bagels, preheat the oven to 450°F.

Recipe continues on next page . . .

In a large saucepan over high heat, bring a pot of water to boil. Place 3 or 4 bagels in boiling water leaving enough room so the bagels aren't touching. Boil on each side for 30 seconds. Remove bagels from water, drain, and return to the sheet pan. Repeat with the remaining bagels.

Bake for 10 to 14 minutes until golden brown. Remove from the oven and let cool.

TO MAKE THE PIZZA BAGELS:

Preheat the oven to 350°F.

Slice the bagels horizontally and place them, cut side up, on a baking sheet.

Divide the tomato sauce equally among the bagels, then sprinkle with the oregano, salt, pepper, and red pepper, if desired. Top with the cheese.

Bake for 8 to 10 minutes until cheese is golden brown. Serve hot.

JERRY'S "DATES"

PREP TIME: 15 MINUTES • COOK TIME: 30 MINUTES • YIELD: 24 PIECES

"Jerry, you break up with a girl every week," says Elaine, and she's right. So let's pay tribute to Jerome Seinfeld's rotating door of companions and fleeting romances. You'll never dump *these* dates though. Why? Well, for starters, they're wrapped in bacon. That's right, "they're real and they're spectacular."

1 pound bacon, sliced

24 Medjool dates, pitted

½ cup blue cheese

Preheat the oven to 400°F.

Cut each slice of bacon in half vertically into about 4-inch strips.

Using a paring knife, slice open each date lengthwise to create space to stuff it. Do not cut all the way through.

Stuff each date with blue cheese, pressing firmly so the cheese stays inside.

Wrap each stuffed date with a strip of bacon.

Place the dates on a baking sheet lined with parchment paper, making sure the seam of the bacon is underneath the dates.

Bake for 15 minutes, then flip and bake another 15 minutes until bacon is crispy. Serve hot or at room temperature.

THESE PRETZELS WILL MAKE YOU THIRSTY

PREP TIME: 30 MINUTES PLUS 10 MINUTES RESTING TIME
COOK TIME: 20 MINUTES • YIELD: 10 PRETZELS

"Are you gonna say it like THAT?" Deliver the line however you'd like, but one thing we do suggest is to have some Snapple on hand for the experience. That's it. Enjoy. If you don't understand the inspiration behind this recipe, return this book to Bob Sacamano immediately.

1½ cups warm water

1 packet instant yeast

1 teaspoon salt

1 tablespoon unsalted butter, melted and cooled

4 cups flour plus more for kneading

¾ cup baking soda

Sea salt

Preheat the oven to 400°F.

Combine the warm water and yeast in a large bowl. Add salt, butter, and flour. Mix until the dough isn't sticky.

On a floured surface, knead the dough for 5 minutes. Then let it rest, covered, for 10 minutes.

Divide the dough into 10 sections. Roll each section into a long rope, then fold into a pretzel shape.

Bring a medium pot of water to a boil and add baking soda. Boil pretzels for about 30 seconds, then let excess water drip off. Place pretzels on a cookie sheet and sprinkle with sea salt, to taste.

Bake for 15 to 17 minutes until browned.

HAND MODEL HAND PIES

PREP TIME: 40 MINUTES • COOK TIME: 25 MINUTES • YIELD: 12 PIES

When Estelle Costanza learns her son may have a potentially lucrative new career, she makes an astute observation about his hands: They're "so soft and milky-white." Though George may be his successor in the hand modeling industry, Ray McKigney would indeed be proud of this entry. Warning: Though decadently delicious, reaching for these treats too many times could have unwelcome side effects for any aspiring hand model. No one should have to depend on Cub Scouts to be fed.

4 tablespoons unsalted butter

½ medium yellow onion, diced

1 carrot, peeled and diced

1 stalk celery, diced

2 teaspoons fresh thyme leaves

1 teaspoon fresh rosemary, minced

½ teaspoon salt

½ teaspoon pepper

2 tablespoons flour

1 cup chicken stock

½ cup milk

1 cup shredded cooked chicken

4 sheets premade pie dough

2 eggs, beaten

Melt the butter in a large skillet over medium heat. Add the onion, carrot, and celery. Cook for 7 to 8 minutes until the vegetables start to soften.

Add the thyme, rosemary, salt, and pepper, then whisk in the flour. Cook for another 2 minutes, taking care not to burn the flour. Add the chicken stock and stir to incorporate, then slowly stir in the milk. Don't add too quickly, or the milk will curdle.

Add the shredded chicken and cook until the sauce thickens, about 3 minutes. Set aside and let cool.

Preheat the oven to 375°F.

Line a baking sheet with foil or parchment paper.

Roll out the pie dough. Cut out twenty-four 4-inch dough circles. Lay out twelve circles on two baking sheets. Brush the outermost ½ inch of the circles with egg, then place 3 tablespoons of the vegetable filling in the center of each one.

Place another dough circle on top of the filling, pinch the edges shut all around with a fork, and pierce the top of each a few times to vent.

Brush the top of each pie with beaten egg.

Bake until golden brown, about 25 minutes. Remove from the oven and serve warm.

CHAPTER 4

NO SOUP FOR YOU

"Is that lima bean?" —Elaine
"Yes." —The Soup Nazi (disgustedly)
"Never been a big fan. Ugh ugh." —Elaine
"THE SOUP NAZI," SEASON 7

Shift into "soup mode" with these ideas sure to warm up any day or ice-cold stoic, no-nonsense personality out there, even that of Yev Kassem himself. Honestly, Elaine should have known better. There are rules when you're in someone else's kitchen, ESPECIALLY the Soup Nazi's. A suggestion for preparations in your domain: Don't forget the bread. In the long run, the embarrassment will cost much more than $3.00.

NEWMAN'S JAMBALAYA

PREP TIME: 15 MINUTES • COOK TIME: 40 MINUTES • YIELD: 8 SERVINGS

Try not to yell "JAMBALAYA!" too loudly after getting a whiff of this sensational soup. You may even take off running down a sidewalk, just like postal employee Newman upon first experiencing the alluring aroma.

2 tablespoons neutral cooking oil

2 andouille sausages (about 12 ounces), thinly sliced

1 medium yellow onion, chopped

2 stalks celery, chopped

1 red bell pepper, chopped

4 cloves garlic, chopped

1 teaspoon garlic powder

1 teaspoon paprika

1 teaspoon salt

½ teaspoon black pepper

½ teaspoon cayenne pepper

4 cups chicken broth

2 cups water

½ cup white rice

One 14-ounce can crushed tomatoes

1 bay leaf

In a stockpot, heat the oil over medium heat. Cook the sausage for about 5 minutes until browned. Transfer to a bowl.

In the same pot, cook the onion, celery, red bell pepper, and garlic until the onion is translucent, about 8 minutes. Add the spices, broth, water, rice, tomatoes, and bay leaf. Cook for 15 minutes, then remove the bay leaf.

Add the sausage back in and cook for another 10 minutes.

Remove from the heat and serve.

ELAINE'S MULLIGATAWNY SOUP

PREP TIME: 20 MINUTES • COOK TIME: 1 HOUR • YIELD: 8 TO 10 SERVINGS

Though clueless as to how to conduct herself in the presence of the eccentric genius known as the Soup Nazi, Elaine's order during the famous episode is unforgettable. For example, he does NOT need to know he looks like Al Pacino. But this time, feel free to tap away on the kitchen counter during preparations. After all, it is your restaurant.

2 cups dried red lentils

12 cups vegetable broth

4 cups water

1 large onion, chopped

4 large cloves garlic, minced

1 tablespoon grated fresh ginger

2 medium carrots, chopped

2 stalks celery, thinly sliced

2 Granny Smith apples, peeled, cored, and chopped

¼ teaspoon ground cinnamon

¼ teaspoon ground cloves

2 teaspoons ground coriander

1 teaspoon ground turmeric

1 teaspoon curry powder

1 tablespoon salt

½ cup finely chopped cilantro, for garnish

Thoroughly rinse lentils in clear water and drain off any excess liquid.

In a large stockpot, add the vegetable broth and water and bring to a boil. Add lentils and cook for 5 minutes.

Add the onion, garlic, ginger, carrots, celery, apples, cinnamon, cloves, coriander, turmeric, curry powder, and salt. Bring to a boil again and then reduce heat. Simmer for about 45 minutes. The liquid in the pot should reduce by about a quarter. Adjust spices to taste.

Serve hot, garnished with cilantro.

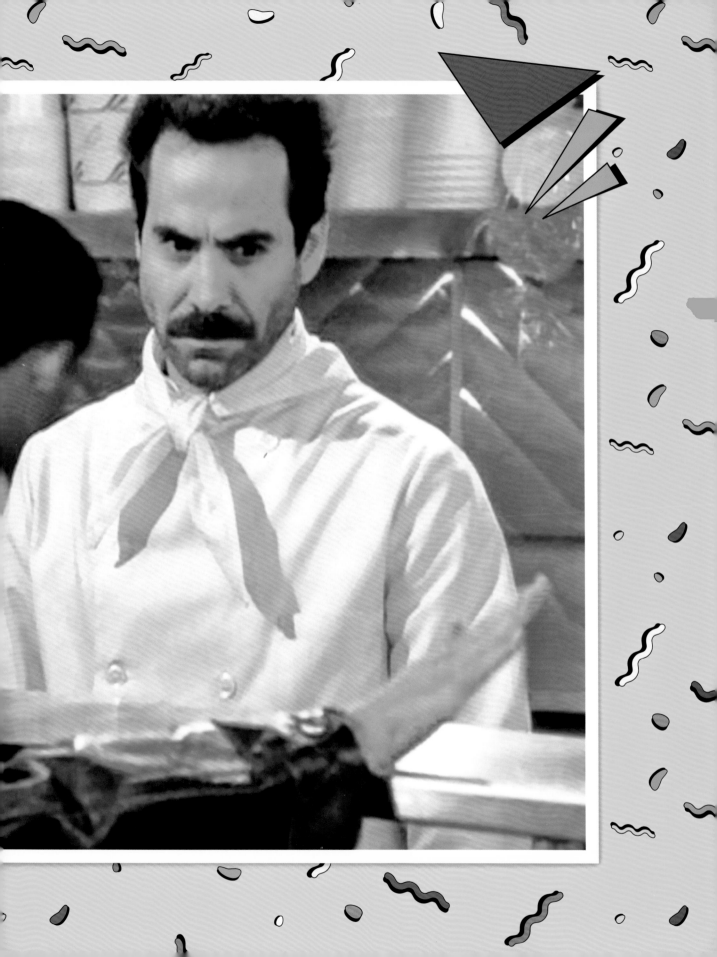

GEORGE'S TURKEY CHILI

PREP TIME: 20 MINUTES • COOK TIME: 55 MINUTES • YIELD: 8 SERVINGS

"You're pushing your luck, little man" is all we can say if you're considering prepping this and something else at the same time. Though George enjoys it, a good turkey chili rivaling that of the Soup Nazi himself will require patience, calmness, and some time—qualities Mr. Costanza does not possess. But we know you do, so get to work.

1 tablespoon neutral cooking oil

2½ pounds ground turkey

2 medium yellow onions, chopped

3 large celery stalks, chopped

½ large red bell pepper, seeded and chopped

5 cloves garlic, minced

1 jalapeno pepper, seeded and chopped

1 poblano pepper, seeded and chopped

1 tablespoon chopped fresh oregano

1 tablespoon chopped fresh parsley

3 tablespoons chili powder

1 teaspoon cayenne pepper

1 teaspoon ground cumin

One 28-ounce can crushed tomatoes

One 28-ounce can diced tomatoes

1 cup chicken broth

One 15-ounce can red kidney beans, drained

1 teaspoon salt

1 teaspoon black pepper

Shredded cheddar cheese, for garnish

Sour cream, for garnish

Heat the oil in a large stockpot over medium-high heat. Add the ground turkey and cook until there's no pink at all, about 12 minutes, taking care to break up any larger pieces.

Add the onions, celery, red pepper, and garlic. Cook until the vegetables soften, about 10 minutes.

Add the remaining peppers, herbs, spices and salt and pepper. Stir to combine and cook another 2 minutes.

Add the tomatoes and broth and bring to a boil. Reduce the heat to medium-low and simmer for 10 minutes.

Add the beans and simmer another 20 minutes. Adjust the spices, but keep in mind the flavors will develop over time. You may want to make the chili a day in advance and let it rest in the refrigerator.

Serve hot, garnished with cheddar cheese and sour cream.

YEV'S BLACK BEAN SOUP

PREP TIME: 20 MINUTES • COOK TIME: 45 MINUTES • YIELD: 6 TO 8 SERVINGS

"ADIOS MUCHACHO" to any so-called *Seinfeld* expert friend if they don't realize that this soup is not actually ordered by anyone in the episode. Only astute *Seinfeld* viewers will note its presence on the menu in the Soup Nazi's lair.

2 tablespoons neutral cooking oil

2 large yellow onions, chopped

3 stalks celery, chopped

1 large carrot, chopped

6 garlic cloves, minced

3 teaspoons ground cumin

1 teaspoon ground coriander

½ teaspoon crushed red pepper

Four 15-ounce cans black beans, rinsed and drained

4 cups vegetable stock

¼ cup fresh cilantro, chopped

Juice of 2 limes

½ teaspoon salt

½ teaspoon black pepper

Sliced avocado, for garnish

Sliced radishes, for garnish

Sour cream, for garnish

In a large stockpot over medium heat, heat the oil. Add the onions, celery, carrot, and garlic. Cook until soft, about 10 minutes.

Add the cumin, coriander, and red pepper. Cook for another 1 minute.

Add the beans and stock and bring to a simmer. Cook for 20 minutes.

Using an immersion blender, blend the soup so the liquid thickens but much of the texture of the vegetables remains.

Add the cilantro, lime juice, salt, and pepper. Adjust the spices to taste. Simmer another 10 minutes to allow the flavors to combine.

Serve with garnishes or without, depending on your preference.

YEV'S MUSHROOM BARLEY SOUP

PREP TIME: 20 MINUTES • COOK TIME: 1 HOUR 20 MINUTES • YIELD: 8 SERVINGS

"COME BACK ONE YEAR!" is the sentence you'll hand down if these same *Seinfeld* veterans don't know that this variety also is not ordered during the episode. But it's included on the Soup Nazi's menu looming in the background.

16 cups vegetable stock

1 cup pearl barley

4 tablespoons neutral cooking oil, divided

1 large onion, chopped

4 stalks celery, chopped

4 large carrots, chopped

4 cloves garlic, minced

1 pound baby bella mushrooms, sliced

6 ounces shiitake mushrooms, sliced

1 teaspoon dried thyme

Salt

Pepper

In a large stockpot over medium-high heat, combine the stock and barley and bring to a simmer. Cook for 30 minutes and continue simmering while you prepare the rest of the soup.

In a large skillet over medium heat, heat 2 tablespoons oil, then add the onion. Cook until translucent, about 8 minutes. Add the celery and carrots and cook until the vegetables are soft, another 8 to 10 minutes. Add the garlic and cook 1 additional minute.

Transfer the vegetables to the stockpot.

In the same skillet, heat the remaining 2 tablespoons of oil over medium-high heat. Add half of the baby bellas and cook without stirring, about 2 minutes. Stir and then cook for another 2 minutes. Add the mushrooms to the soup.

Repeat with the remaining baby bellas and the shiitake mushrooms.

Add the thyme and salt and pepper to taste. Simmer another 20 minutes. The soup will thicken and become more flavorful as it cooks and cools.

YEV'S CHICKEN BROCCOLI SOUP

PREP TIME: 15 MINUTES • COOK TIME: 45 MINUTES • YIELD: 6 TO 8 SERVINGS

See our entries for "Yev's Black Bean Soup" and "Yev's Mushroom Barley Soup." Act accordingly. On that note, as Elaine would say, "NEXT!"

2 tablespoons unsalted butter

1 medium onion, minced

2 large carrots, minced

2 cups broccoli, finely chopped

6 cups chicken stock

2 cups cooked chicken, shredded

1 teaspoon kosher salt

1 teaspoon pepper

1 cup heavy cream, or milk

2 cups shredded sharp cheddar

In a large stockpot over medium heat, melt the butter. Add the onion and cook until translucent, about 8 minutes.

Add the carrots and broccoli. Cook for another 5 minutes, until vegetables start to soften.

Add the stock, shredded chicken, salt, and pepper. Simmer for 20 minutes.

While the soup is cooking, heat the cream and cheddar cheese in a small saucepan over medium-low heat, whisking often, until the cheese is melted and the mixture is smooth. Add the cheese mixture to the soup.

Simmer for another 10 minutes and adjust spices to taste. Serve hot.

YADA YADA YADA
LOBSTER BISQUE

PREP TIME: 15 MINUTES • COOK TIME: 40 MINUTES • YIELD: 4 TO 6 SERVINGS

Oh, you'll "mention the bisque!" You won't yada yada over this one, because, quite simply, it's the best part of this chapter. Just don't tell the Soup Nazi. He'll ban you.

4 tablespoons unsalted butter, divided

2 scallions, diced

3 large stalks celery, diced

3 large carrots peeled, diced

1 tablespoon salt

1 tablespoon pepper

5 cloves garlic, minced

1 tablespoon chopped fresh thyme

3 tablespoons flour

3 tablespoons tomato paste

1 cup medium sherry

4 cups seafood stock

1 teaspoon smoked paprika

¼ teaspoon ground cayenne pepper

1 cup heavy cream

1 pound cooked lobster meat, chopped

2 tablespoons chopped parsley, for garnish

Melt 2 tablespoons butter in a large stockpot over medium heat. Add the scallions and cook for 2 minutes until they begin to soften. Add the celery, carrots, salt, and pepper. Cook until the vegetables begin to soften, about 6 minutes. Add the garlic and thyme and cook another 2 minutes. Turn off the heat.

In a medium saucepan over medium-low heat, make a roux. Melt the remaining 2 tablespoons of butter, then whisk in the flour and continue whisking until the flour is golden brown. (Roux is easy to burn because it needs constant attention. If you burn this or your roux is very dark brown, start over.)

Reduce heat to low, add tomato paste, and whisk until smooth, then whisk in the sherry, seafood stock, paprika, and cayenne pepper.

Add the liquids to your stockpot. Using an immersion blender, blend the mixture until smooth, then stir in the cream, add the lobster meat, and adjust the spices.

Bring the soup to a simmer over medium heat and cook for 10 minutes. Serve hot, garnished with parsley.

CHAPTER 5

MONK'S CAFE

"I really do like this coffee shop!" —Jerry

"THE SOUP," SEASON 6

Over the years, the gang regularly meets at the coffee shop to plan, scheme, and discuss subtle nuances, petty nonsense, and all aspects of their lives. Now it's possible to make any location a Monk's with these café-themed ideas. Rules are out the window, so you can even bring in outside condiments. They won't be confiscated, because Larry will never know. We promise.

GEORGE'S BEDROOM PASTRAMI

PREP TIME: 5 MINUTES • COOK TIME: 5 MINUTES • YIELD: 4 SANDWICHES

"You've combined food and sex into one disgusting, uncontrollable urge!" Though we, personally, don't recommend eating this from under the covers (but that's personal business), we do think you'll enjoy this one inspired by our balding friend. Is it "the most sensual of all the salted-cured meats"? Possibly. Ask George. Or Vivian. If you can pull them away from each other.

½ cup water, or beef stock

3 pounds thinly sliced pastrami

¼ cup spicy brown mustard, divided

8 slices marble rye (see page 39)

In a large skillet over medium-low heat, warm the water or stock, then add the pastrami. Cover with a lid and let steam for about 5 minutes, stirring occasionally, until warm. Remove from the heat and keep covered.

Divide the mustard and spread on all 8 slices of bread.

Using tongs, remove pastrami from skillet, allowing extra liquid to drip off, then divide evenly among 4 slices of bread. Top with remaining 4 bread slices.

Cut each sandwich in half and serve.

JERRY'S VEGETABLE SANDWICH

PREP TIME: 15 MINUTES • YIELD: 4 SANDWICHES

"Thanks for mutton," indeed. Want to turn into a "healthy person" like Jerry as he orders this at Monk's to change up his diet? This one might eventually help you fit into those size 31 waist jeans, even without buying a size up and crossing off the "2." A quick word to the wise: "PULP CAN MOVE, BABY!" So be careful when adding a side of grapefruit. Just ask George.

2 ripe avocados

Juice of ½ lemon

½ teaspoon red pepper flakes

¼ teaspoon salt

¼ teaspoon pepper

1 cucumber

2 medium carrots

8 slices whole wheat bread

8 pitted kalamata olives, halved

One 4-ounce brick feta cheese, drained

4 leaves romaine lettuce, trimmed into 8 sandwich-sized pieces

Using a paring knife, make a vertical cut all the way around the outside of each avocado, stopping when you hit the large pit inside. Pull the halves apart and discard the pits. Scoop out the flesh into a small mixing bowl.

Add the lemon juice, red pepper flakes, salt, and pepper and combine well. Adjust the spices to taste. Set aside.

Slice the cucumber into thin rounds. Set aside.

Trim the ends of the carrots. Using a vegetable peeler, make long, thin strips of carrot. To save your fingertips, use a fork to hold down the carrots.

Toast the whole wheat bread. Spread one-quarter of the avocado mixture onto 1 slice of toasted bread, then top with one-quarter of the cucumber slices, carrot strips, and halved olives. Cut the feta cheese into 4 equal slices and add 1 feta slice and 2 pieces of lettuce to the sandwich. Top with another slice of toast, then cut diagonally in half.

Repeat with the other three sandwiches and serve.

JERRY'S EGG WHITE OMELET

PREP TIME: 10 MINUTES • COOK TIME: 10 MINUTES • YIELD: 2 SERVINGS

Thankfully, this isn't REGGIE'S, so there's no need to panic and order a Western (or be forced to order Sanka). We have the recipe for Jerry's preference right here, and we will not be visiting the Bizarro world today. Our apologies to Gene, Kevin, and Feldman.

6 egg whites, divided

Salt

Pepper

½ cup chopped cooked vegetables (like tomatoes, green and red peppers, broccoli, or spinach), divided

2 ounces cooked bacon, crumbled, divided

¼ cup shredded cheese, divided

In a medium bowl, whisk the egg whites until frothy, about 2 minutes.

Spray a small skillet with nonstick cooking spray and heat over medium heat. Add half the egg whites and cook until they start to turn opaque, about 1 to 2 minutes. Using a spatula, lift a side and allow uncooked egg whites to run underneath. Season with salt and pepper and add half the vegetables, bacon, and cheese. Fold over and transfer to a plate.

Repeat with the remaining egg whites, vegetables, bacon, and cheese.

Plate and serve hot.

ELAINE'S BIG SALAD

PREP TIME: 15 MINUTES • YIELD: 2 SERVINGS

"Tomatoes like volleyballs?" They could work. Elaine's favorite is sure to indulge the salad lover in your life. This is so much better than two small salads offered by Hildy. No comparison.

FOR THE DRESSING
Juice of 1 small lemon

1½ tablespoons Dijon mustard

¼ cup extra-virgin olive oil

¾ teaspoon sea salt

½ teaspoon pepper

FOR THE SALAD
1 large head iceberg lettuce, shredded

1 ripe avocado

2 hard-boiled eggs

4 strips cooked bacon, crumbled

1 cup shredded cooked chicken

½ cup grape tomatoes, halved

½ cup crumbled blue cheese

TO MAKE THE DRESSING:

Combine all ingredients into a small mixing bowl and whisk vigorously to emulsify. Adjust the seasonings to taste. You may want to add more lemon juice depending on how flavorful your olive oil is. Set aside.

TO MAKE THE SALAD:

Evenly divide the lettuce between two large salad bowls.

Using a paring knife, make a vertical cut all the way around the outside of the avocado, stopping when you hit the large pit inside. Pull the halves apart and discard the pit. While the flesh is still inside the skin, score the avocado meat into slices, then scoop out using a large spoon. Set aside.

Peel the hard-boiled eggs and slice into quarters. Set aside.

Divide the salad toppings in half and arrange them in the two salads so that each one is displayed individually on the lettuce: Designate separate areas for the avocado slices, bacon crumbles, shredded chicken, eggs, tomatoes, and blue cheese.

Top each salad with dressing and serve.

GEORGE'S USUAL: TUNA ON TOAST

PREP TIME: 15 MINUTES • YIELD: 4 SANDWICHES

If you're like George, well, we're sorry. But more importantly, nothing has ever worked out by ordering tuna on toast. Salute the self-proclaimed "Costanza, Lord of the Idiots" or totally change things up and make the opposite: chicken salad on rye. Or is it salmon? You decide.

Two 6-ounce cans white meat tuna, drained

1 medium stalk celery, minced

⅓ cup mayonnaise

2 tablespoons Dijon mustard

1 teaspoon celery salt

½ teaspoon pepper

Squeeze of lemon juice

8 slices white bread

4 leaves lettuce, trimmed into 8 sandwich-size pieces

In a medium bowl, combine the tuna, celery, mayonnaise, mustard, celery salt, pepper, and lemon juice. Stir well, breaking up any large chunks of tuna. Adjust the spices to taste.

Toast the bread to golden brown.

Place one piece of lettuce on a slice of bread, then top with one-quarter of the tuna mixture. Top with another piece of toasted bread and cut diagonally in half.

Repeat to make the other three sandwiches and serve.

THE OPPOSITE OF TUNA ON TOAST

PREP TIME: 15 MINUTES • YIELD: 4 SANDWICHES

"Chicken salad, on rye, untoasted, . . . and a cup of tea!" As we were saying, we went with chicken salad. The bottom line here is, when making this dish, be prepared for attention from women named Victoria or a job offer from the New York Yankees. Though neither are guaranteed.

4 cups shredded cooked chicken

1 cup mayonnaise

2 teaspoons lemon juice

2 tablespoons Dijon mustard

1 small stalk celery, minced

½ small red onion, minced

2 tablespoons fresh dill, minced

½ teaspoon salt

½ teaspoon pepper

4 lettuce leaves, trimmed into 8 sandwich-size pieces

4 bulkie rolls

In a medium mixing bowl, combine the shredded chicken, mayonnaise, lemon juice, Dijon mustard, celery, red onion, dill, salt, and pepper. Adjust seasonings to taste.

Slice each roll horizontally. Add one piece of lettuce, one-quarter of the chicken salad, and another piece of lettuce, then close the sandwich and slice.

Repeat to assemble the other three sandwiches and serve.

CHAPTER 6

TAKEOUT

"Is there a captain's hat involved in all this?" —Jerry
"Maybe." —Elaine
"THE STRIKE," SEASON 9

It takes a disturbing level of dedication to earn Elaine that elusive free sandwich at Atomic Sub. That same indomitable spirit is also on display as she creates a fake apartment in order to get her Supreme Flounder delivery. But really, all of our heroes know their way around New York's food scene. From chicken to calzones and more, the gang always knows the spots and selections for fast food, or as Jerry's old friend, Seth, refers to it, "good food quickly." Here, now, is your chance to eat just like them. You can even dine like Mr. Steinbrenner and George at lunch and won't even need Newman's help.

KRAMER WANTS A PAPAYA KING HOT DOG

PREP TIME: 5 MINUTES • COOK TIME: 40 MINUTES • YIELD: 4 HOT DOGS

Don't insult Kramer's intelligence by suggesting any other hot dog—there's just no comparison. Instead, indulge the K-Man's love of this one by making a Papaya King–style hot dog for your own enjoyment. Trust us, it tastes even better before heading to a movie theater to see *Checkmate*.

FOR THE ONION SAUCE

2 tablespoons neutral cooking oil

2 medium onions, thinly sliced

1 teaspoon chili powder

½ teaspoon smoked paprika

½ teaspoon salt

½ teaspoon ground pepper

1 cup water

½ cup ketchup

1 teaspoon hot sauce

FOR THE HOT DOGS

2 tablespoons neutral cooking oil

4 New York–style frankfurters

4 hot dog rolls

Sauerkraut (optional)

Pickle relish (optional)

TO MAKE THE ONION SAUCE:

Heat the oil in a medium skillet over medium heat. Add the onions and cook until softened, about 8 minutes.

Add the chili powder, paprika, salt, and pepper. Cook for 1 minute.

Add water, ketchup, and hot sauce and simmer until the sauce is thick and the onions are very soft, about 20 minutes. Set aside.

TO MAKE THE HOT DOGS:

On a griddle, heat the oil over medium-high heat. Grill the frankfurters until browned on all sides, about 5 to 6 minutes. Remove from pan.

Place hot dog rolls, split side-down, on the griddle and heat for about 1 to 2 minutes until lightly browned. Remove from the heat.

To assemble the hot dogs, place one frankfurter in each bun, then top with onion sauce and sauerkraut and relish, if desired. Serve hot.

STEINBRENNER SPECIAL CALZONE

PREP TIME: 1 HOUR PLUS 1 HOUR RESTING TIME • COOK TIME: 40 MINUTES
YIELD: TWO 12-INCH CALZONES

"Big Stein wants an eggplant calzone!" After checking out this recipe, he won't be the only one! Concerned about making a mess? Don't be. "The pita pocket prevents it from dripping. The pita pocket!" What's not to love?

FOR THE PIZZA DOUGH
1 packet instant yeast

1 ¾ cups warm water

4 tablespoons olive oil, divided

1 teaspoon kosher salt

½ teaspoon granulated sugar

5 cups bread flour plus more if needed

FOR THE CALZONES
1 medium eggplant

6 cups water plus 2 tablespoons, divided

1 tablespoon kosher salt

1 cup all-purpose flour

2 eggs, beaten

2 cups Italian bread crumbs

¼ cup neutral cooking oil, divided

¾ cup pizza sauce

1 cup shredded mozzarella

½ cup pepperoni

8 slices provolone cheese

2 tablespoons olive oil

¼ cup grated Parmesan cheese

1 teaspoon Italian seasoning

TO MAKE THE PIZZA DOUGH:

In the bowl of a mixer fitted with a dough hook, combine the yeast, warm water, 3 tablespoons of olive oil, salt, and sugar. While mixer is running on low, slowly add the flour to the bowl over the course of 2 minutes.

Increase speed to medium and knead for 6 to 8 minutes until a firm ball forms that pulls away from the sides of the bowl. If the dough is very sticky, add a few tablespoons of flour. If the dough is too dry, add a tablespoon of water.

Remove dough from mixer, then cut in half. Coat both dough balls with the remaining 1 tablespoon of olive oil, then cover and allow to rest for at least 30 minutes or up to an hour.

TO MAKE THE CALZONES:

While the dough is resting, peel the eggplant and slice it into ¼-inch rounds. Fill a large mixing bowl with 6 cups of water and stir in the salt. Immerse the eggplant slices in the water for at least 10 minutes to draw out the bitterness. Drain the eggplant and pat dry.

Using three small bowls, set up an assembly line. In one, place the flour; in the second bowl, the eggs and 2 tablespoons water; and in the third bowl, the bread crumbs. Dredge each slice of eggplant in flour on both sides, then shake off excess. Next, submerge the eggplant slice in the egg mixture and allow it to drip for a moment before dredging it through the bread crumbs. Repeat with all the eggplant slices and set aside.

Heat 2 tablespoons of oil in a large skillet over medium-high heat. When the oil is hot, place about 4 slices of prepared eggplant into the pan, making sure no slices are touching. Cook until golden brown, about 3 to 4 minutes per side, and remove to a paper towel–lined plate to drain. Repeat with the remaining eggplant slices, adding more oil as needed.

Recipe continues on next page . . .

Preheat the oven to 475°F.

On a lightly floured surface, roll out each dough ball to a 12-inch disc. If the dough shrinks back, allow it to rest briefly before rolling it further.

Assemble the calzones. You're going to want to put toppings on only half of the dough, leaving at least a ½-inch circumference around the outer edge. Spread 2 tablespoons of pizza sauce on one half of a dough circle, then top the sauce with ¼ cup mozzarella. Add 2 or 3 slices of eggplant, 2 more tablespoons of sauce, one-quarter of the pepperoni, and 2 slices of provolone. Repeat with more eggplant, sauce, pepperoni, and provolone. Top with another ¼ cup of mozzarella.

Carefully fold the dough over the toppings to make a half-circle, pressing down firmly on the edges to seal the filling inside.

Repeat assembly process to make the other calzone.

Brush the tops of the calzones with olive oil and score their tops with a few small cuts to vent the steam. Top each calzone with half the Parmesan cheese and Italian seasoning.

Bake for 12 to 15 minutes until golden brown and serve.

ACROSS THE STREET
SUPREME FLOUNDER

PREP TIME: 10 MINUTES • COOK TIME: 15 MINUTES • YIELD: 4 SERVINGS

We are unable to guarantee that the delivery driver will come to your neighborhood, or even to your side of the street. So you'll have to do it yourself. To truly complete the Elaine experience, find a supply closet and eat inside, but don't invite any friends. One—like Kramer—might spill some ammonia and ruin everything. Although, as Elaine says, "It's better than eating it alone in the restaurant, like some loser."

One 1-pound flounder, or 1 pound of whitefish filets

¼ cup cornstarch

½ teaspoon salt

½ teaspoon pepper

½ cup neutral cooking oil

3 cloves garlic, minced

2 tablespoons fresh ginger, minced

2 scallions, chopped

2 tablespoons water

2 tablespoons soy sauce

½ teaspoon sugar

1 tablespoon Shaoxing wine

¼ cup chopped fresh cilantro

If you're using a whole fish for this recipe, as is the traditional Chinese preparation, have your fishmonger clean the fish of scales and inner organs but leave the fins and head in place. Pat whole fish or filets dry.

In a small bowl, combine the cornstarch, salt, and pepper. Coat both sides of the fish evenly with mixture and shake off any excess.

In a wok or large skillet over medium-high heat, heat the oil until a few droplets of water dropped on the surface sizzle. Fry the fish until golden brown, about 5 minutes per side for the whole fish and slightly less for the filets depending on their thickness. Flip just once to keep the fish intact.

Remove fish to a platter and cover with foil to keep warm.

Drain all but 2 tablespoons of oil from the skillet, removing any bits of fish, and return the skillet to a medium flame. Add the garlic, ginger, and scallions and cook for 2 minutes.

Add the water, soy sauce, sugar, and wine. Cook for 1 minute.

Spoon the sauce over the fish, garnish with cilantro, and serve.

ELAINE'S SUBMARINE CAPTAIN SUB

PREP TIME: 5 MINUTES • YIELD: 2 SANDWICHES

We have no doubt that many readers, much like Elaine herself, have "eaten a lot of CRAP" to get to where they are today. Though she never claimed her free sub and captain's hat, we can honor her laborious journey through twenty-four subs to attain the ranking of *Seinfeld* Submarine Captain.

FOR THE VINAIGRETTE

¼ cup red wine vinegar

¼ cup olive oil

1 tablespoon dried parsley

Salt

Pepper

FOR THE SUBS

2 submarine sandwich rolls

6 slices salami

6 slices mortadella

6 slices capicola

6 slices ham

6 slices prosciutto

6 slices provolone

½ cup shredded iceberg lettuce

1 small tomato, sliced

TO MAKE THE VINAIGRETTE:

In a small bowl, combine the vinegar, olive oil, parsley, salt, and pepper. Whisk to combine and adjust spices to taste.

TO MAKE THE SUBS:

Slice the sandwich rolls lengthwise, leaving the halves attached. Drizzle the insides of each one with half the vinaigrette.

Layer half of the meats and cheeses in each roll, then top with lettuce and tomato slices.

Drizzle the remaining vinaigrette over the filling and serve.

KENNY'S ROASTER CHICKEN

PREP TIME: 10 MINUTES PLUS OVERNIGHT MARINATING TIME
COOK TIME: 45 MINUTES TO 1 HOUR PLUS 50 MINUTES RESTING TIME
YIELD: 4 SERVINGS

"The greasy doorknob, the constant licking of the fingers. He's hooked on the chicken, isn't he?" Share the craving since this one is no gamble—it's an absolute winner. Get hooked just like the K-Man, but we can't help with the glowing red light that overpowers the entire apartment.

FOR THE MARINADE
1 teaspoon kosher salt

½ teaspoon pepper

2 tablespoons unsalted butter, melted

1 tablespoon Dijon mustard

Juice of 1 lemon

⅓ cup neutral cooking oil

¼ cup soy sauce

1 tablespoon honey

¼ teaspoon liquid smoke

One 3- to 4-pound whole chicken

FOR THE DRY RUB
2 teaspoons kosher salt

1 teaspoon black pepper

½ teaspoon cayenne pepper

1 teaspoon onion powder

1 teaspoon garlic salt

1 teaspoon smoked paprika

1 teaspoon dried parsley

TO MAKE THE MARINADE AND PREPARE THE CHICKEN:

In a medium mixing bowl, combine the salt, pepper, butter, mustard, lemon juice, oil, soy sauce, honey, and liquid smoke.

Clean the chicken well and pat dry.

Place the chicken in a shallow dish and rub the marinade all over. Cover tightly and refrigerate overnight.

TO MAKE THE DRY RUB AND ROAST THE CHICKEN:

Before roasting, set the wrapped chicken on the counter for half an hour.

Preheat the oven to 350°F.

In a small bowl, combine the salt, pepper, cayenne pepper, onion powder, garlic salt, paprika, and parsley.

Unwrap the chicken, spooning any extra marinade inside. Rub the dry rub all over the outside of the chicken.

Roast uncovered for 15 minutes per pound, until the juices run clear when you make a cut between the leg and thigh.

Remove the chicken from the oven and allow to rest for 20 minutes before carving.

PUDDY'S FAVORITE SANDWICH

PREP TIME: 5 MINUTES • COOK TIME: 15 MINUTES • YIELD: 4 SANDWICHES

"Feels like an Arby's night." If so, this option will channel the Puddy in all of us. A few words of caution, however. Consuming it too fast may cause permanent eye squinting and sudden, arbitrary face painting during NHL playoff season.

FOR THE SAUCE

¼ cup water

½ cup ketchup

2 tablespoons dark brown sugar

2 tablespoons apple cider vinegar

¼ teaspoon onion powder

¼ teaspoon garlic powder

¼ teaspoon cayenne pepper

1 tablespoon Worcestershire sauce

¼ teaspoon kosher salt

FOR THE SANDWICHES

½ cup water, or beef stock

2 pounds lean roast beef, cooked and thinly sliced

4 seeded sandwich buns

TO MAKE THE SAUCE:

Combine all ingredients in a small saucepan and bring to a simmer over medium heat.

Cook for 10 minutes until the sauce thickens slightly. Set aside.

TO MAKE THE SANDWICHES:

In a large skillet over medium-low heat, warm the water or stock, then add the roast beef. Cover with a lid and let steam for about 5 minutes until warm, stirring occasionally. Remove from the heat and keep covered.

Toast the sandwich buns.

Divide the roast beef equally among the 4 sandwich bun bottoms, then spoon sauce over each one.

Top with the sandwich bun tops and serve.

LONG WAIT LO MEIN

PREP TIME: 10 MINUTES • COOK TIME: 15 MINUTES • YIELD: 4 SERVINGS

Though this will take longer than "5 to 10 minutes," it'll be worth the wait. Just don't give up and go to Sky Burger. Be patient, hang in there, and trust that eventually they will call your name. Cartwright would want you to, but that begs the question, "Who's Cartwright?"

FOR THE SAUCE
3 tablespoons soy sauce

1 tablespoon granulated sugar

2 teaspoons sesame oil

1 tablespoon grated ginger

1 teaspoon garlic-chili hot sauce

1½ tablespoons cornstarch

1½ tablespoons rice wine

FOR THE LO MEIN
One 14-ounce package lo mein
   noodles

1 tablespoon neutral cooking oil

4 cloves garlic, minced

1 medium onion, finely sliced

2 cups mushrooms, sliced

1 red bell pepper, julienned

1 carrot, julienned

½ cup snow peas, trimmed

3 cups bok choy, chopped

TO MAKE THE SAUCE:
In a small bowl, whisk together all ingredients until the cornstarch is dissolved. Taste and adjust the flavors to your liking, adding more hot sauce for a spicier sauce or more sesame oil and rice wine for a milder one. Set aside.

TO MAKE THE LO MEIN:
Cook the noodles according to package directions and drain.

While the noodles are cooking, heat the oil over medium-high heat in a large skillet or wok. Add the garlic, onion, mushrooms, bell pepper, and carrot. Cook until tender, about 5 minutes. Add the snow peas and bok choy and cook another 3 minutes.

Add the cooked noodles and sauce to the pan and mix well, stirring until the mixture is heated through. Serve immediately.

CHAPTER 7

DINNER

"And you know what you do at dinner?" —Kramer
"What?" —Jerry
"You talk about your day." —Kramer.
"THE ENGAGEMENT," SEASON 7

Notwithstanding Kramer's "insightful" views on matrimony, dinnertime is the Main Event Meal for many. Whether force-feeding yourself a steak at 4:30 p.m. with Jerry's parents at Del Boca Vista to save a couple of bucks or preparing for a candlelight dinner at Pomodoro—even though everyone goes there to break up—the *Seinfeld* universe knows its way around the dinner table with these inspiring selections.

FESTIVUS MEATLOAF

PREP TIME: 10 MINUTES • COOK TIME: 1 HOUR 15 MINUTES TO 1 HOUR 20 MINUTES
YIELD: 6 SERVINGS

A meatloaf for the rest of us! There will be NO airing of grievances when it comes to this masterpiece. In fact, you'll be too stuffed to even THINK about competing in the feats of strength. Simply spend all night with Frank and Estelle Costanza contently staring at an aluminum pole instead. It has a very high strength-to-weight ratio.

FOR THE GLAZE
½ cup tomato paste

¼ cup brown sugar

¼ cup white vinegar

1 teaspoon yellow mustard

FOR THE MEATLOAF
1 pound ground beef

1 pound ground pork

¼ cup grated onion

1 egg

1 cup seasoned bread crumbs

¼ cup tomato paste

1 tablespoon Worcestershire Sauce

1 teaspoon salt

½ teaspoon pepper

1 teaspoon Italian seasoning

1 teaspoon garlic powder

TO MAKE THE GLAZE:
In a medium mixing bowl, combine all ingredients. Set aside.

TO MAKE THE MEATLOAF:
Preheat the oven to 350°F.

Spray a loaf pan with nonstick cooking spray.

In a large bowl, combine all ingredients until well mixed. Place in the loaf pan and top evenly with the glaze.

Bake for 75 to 80 minutes, or until the internal temperature reaches 155°F.

Remove the meatloaf from the oven. Allow to cool slightly, then slice and serve.

JERRY'S "JUST A SALAD"

PREP TIME: 5 MINUTES • YIELD: 4 SERVINGS

"What is mutton anyway?" It's all irrelevant, plus, like Jerry, we don't want to find out. So follow his lead and go with "just a salad," regardless of any looks or half-turns you might get from the wait staff or preferred dining companions.

Juice of 1 small lemon

2 tablespoons white wine vinegar

¼ cup extra-virgin olive oil

¾ teaspoon sea salt

Pepper

8 cups mixed greens

In a small mixing bowl, combine the lemon juice and vinegar.

Whisk in the olive oil until emulsified. Add salt and pepper to taste.

Place the greens in a serving bowl and toss with the dressing. Serve immediately.

FRANCO'S CHOPS

PREP TIME: 10 MINUTES PLUS 30 MINUTES RESTING TIME
COOK TIME: 30 MINUTES • YIELD: 4 SERVINGS

If one develops the irresistible urge to cook pork chops, but their butcher, Franco, is out of town, this recipe will have to suffice. Who needs him anyway? He'd probably act like he didn't know you. That is *so* Franco . . .

FOR THE PORK CHOPS
Four 1-inch-thick pork chops

1 tablespoon all-purpose flour

1 teaspoon salt

1 teaspoon garlic powder

½ teaspoon pepper

2 tablespoons neutral cooking oil

FOR THE DIJON HERB SAUCE
1 tablespoon neutral cooking oil

1 large shallot, thinly sliced

2 tablespoons fresh thyme leaves

1 tablespoon chopped fresh rosemary

2 tablespoons Dijon mustard

Juice of 1 lemon

½ cup chicken stock

½ cup dry white wine

4 tablespoons (1/2 stick) cold unsalted butter, divided

TO MAKE THE PORK CHOPS:

Allow the pork chops to come to room temperature for at least 30 minutes before cooking.

In a small bowl, combine the flour, salt, garlic powder, and pepper. Rub the mixture evenly on both sides of each pork chop.

Heat the oil until hot in a large skillet over medium-high heat. Add the pork chops and sear on one side until lightly browned, about 4 minutes. Reduce heat to low.

Flip the pork chops, then cover skillet with a lid. Cook until a meat thermometer inserted into the thickest part of the chops reads 145°F. This could take 6 to 10 minutes depending on the thickness of your pork chops, so start taking readings at 6 minutes and check periodically afterward.

When fully cooked, transfer pork chops to a platter and cover with aluminum foil. Allow them to rest while you prepare the sauce.

TO MAKE THE DIJON HERB SAUCE:

Heat oil over medium heat in the same pan you used to cook the pork chops. Add the shallot and cook until softened, about 3 minutes. Add the thyme and rosemary and cook 1 more minute. Whisk in the mustard, lemon juice, and chicken stock. Cook for 2 minutes. Add the wine and simmer until sauce is reduced by half, about 5 minutes. Whisk in the butter, 1 tablespoon at a time, until the sauce comes together. Adjust spices to taste.

Spoon the sauce over the pork chops and serve hot.

COSMO'S UNSEEN BOUILLABAISSE

PREP TIME: 40 MINUTES PLUS 30 MINUTES SOAKING TIME
COOK TIME: 60 MINUTES • YIELD: 6 SERVINGS

As Jerry has said about the K-Man, "That nut is always up to something." It's true. When Helen and Morty Seinfeld visit and take over Jerry's apartment, Jerry stays with the hipster doofus himself. How does Kramer welcome Jerry? By making an unseen bouillabaisse. Have a friend visiting? Follow Cosmo's lead and eat like Upper West Side pals.

½ pound littleneck clams, cleaned

4 tablespoons sea salt, divided

¼ cup extra-virgin olive oil

1 medium onion, finely chopped

1 large leek, white and tender green parts only, thinly sliced

2 stalks celery, finely chopped

1 small fennel bulb, thinly sliced

3 cloves garlic, minced

1 cup grape tomatoes, halved

6 cups seafood stock

1 cup dry white wine

6 thyme sprigs

6 rosemary sprigs

½ teaspoon crumbled saffron

1 teaspoon black pepper

½ pound shrimp, peeled and deveined

¾ pound whitefish (like cod or halibut), cut into 1-inch chunks

½ pound scallops

½ pound mussels, cleaned and debearded

In a large bowl, soak the littlenecks in cold water salted with 3 tablespoons sea salt for at least 30 minutes to remove the sand.

In a large stockpot over medium heat, cook the onion, leek, and celery until they soften and start to turn translucent, about 6 minutes. Add the fennel, garlic, and tomatoes and cook another 2 minutes.

Add the seafood stock, wine, thyme and rosemary sprigs, saffron, 1 tablespoon of salt, and pepper. Bring to a boil, then reduce heat and simmer for 30 minutes. (The stock can be made a day in advance and kept in the refrigerator.)

Add the shrimp, whitefish, scallops, and mussels and simmer, covered, for about 10 to 15 minutes, until the shells open.

Serve the soup in large bowls with crusty bread.

MAN-HANDS LOBSTER

PREP TIME: 10 MINUTES • COOK TIME: 40 MINUTES • YIELD: 2 SERVINGS

"She had man hands." With hands like George "The Animal" Steele—or Jerry's current girlfriend, Gillian—break apart this succulent lobster (though we recommend claws). If planning to make a mess, save the napkin and have a beach towel standing by on the rack.

FOR THE HERB BUTTER
½ cup (1 stick) unsalted butter

2 tablespoons fresh dill, minced

2 tablespoons fresh chives, minced

1 teaspoon lemon zest, grated

¼ teaspoon salt

FOR THE LOBSTERS
2 tablespoons salt

Two 1¼- to 1½-pound lobsters

FOR THE HERB BUTTER:

In a small skillet over medium heat, melt the butter. Add the herbs, lemon zest, and salt. Cook for 2 minutes to infuse the flavors into the butter. Remove from the heat and set aside.

TO MAKE THE LOBSTERS:

Fill a large stockpot two-thirds full of water, add salt, and bring to a boil over high heat.

Drop the lobsters in headfirst and cover the pot. Boil until the lobsters' shells are bright red. Cooking time will vary by lobster size but should be about 14 to 18 minutes.

Using tongs, transfer the lobsters to a colander and allow to drain for a few minutes.

If you'd like to make cracking the shells easier, score the lobsters' tails and claws with a sharp kitchen knife before serving.

Rewarm the herb butter, divide into two small bowls, and serve a bowl with each lobster.

MAKE YOUR OWN PIZZA PIE

PREP TIME: 20 MINUTES PLUS 30 MINUTES RISING TIMECOOK TIME: 11 MINUTES • YIELD: FOUR 6-INCH PIZZAS

"You pound it, slap it, you flip it up into the air . . . put your toppings on, and you slide it into the oven!" Giddyap. Cheese? Pepperoni? Cucumbers? Just like Kramer explains, there are no rules when it comes to making your own pizza. Though Poppie may disagree, it's all yours, cowboy.

FOR THE PIZZA DOUGH

1 packet instant yeast

1¾ cups warm water

4 tablespoons olive oil, divided

1 teaspoon kosher salt

½ teaspoon granulated sugar

5 cups bread flour plus 2
   tablespoons more, if needed

¼ cup cornmeal, for dusting

FOR THE PIZZAS

1 cup tomato sauce, divided

2 cups shredded mozzarella,
   divided

½ cup grated Parmesan, divided

½ cup sliced pepperoni, divided

Red pepper flakes (optional)

Kosher salt

Pepper

TO MAKE THE PIZZA DOUGH:

In the bowl of a mixer fitted with a dough hook, combine the yeast, water, 3 tablespoons of olive oil, salt, and sugar. While mixer is running on low, slowly add the flour to the bowl over the course of 2 minutes.

Increase mixer speed to medium and knead dough for 6 to 8 minutes until a firm ball forms that pulls away from the sides of the bowl. If the dough is very sticky, add a few tablespoons of flour. If the dough is too dry, add 1 tablespoon of water.

Remove dough from mixer and cut in quarters. Coat dough balls with the remaining 1 tablespoon of olive oil, then cover and allow to sit for 30 minutes to rest.

TO MAKE THE PIZZAS:

When the dough has rested, preheat the oven to 475°F.

On a lightly floured surface, roll out each dough ball into a 6-inch disc. If the dough shrinks back, allow it to rest briefly before rolling it further.

Dust a cutting board or pizza board with cornmeal, then place the dough discs on top. Divide the tomato sauce, cheeses, and pepperoni evenly between the 4 pizzas and top with red pepper flakes, if desired, and salt and pepper to taste.

Carefully transfer the assembled pizzas to a baking sheet lined with parchment paper.

Bake for 9 to 11 minutes until the crust is golden brown. Serve hot from the oven.

FUSILLI JERRY

PREP TIME: 15 MINUTES • COOK TIME: 45 MINUTES • YIELD: 4 SERVINGS

Why? Because we're silly, like Jerry. Kramer's tribute to his comedian friend had to make this book and could quite possibly be the ultimate *Seinfeld*-themed food homage. We'll tell you where we'd like to put it . . . directly on your plate. If only there was a pasta inspired by George . . .

1 pound store-bought fresh fusilli

One 28-ounce can whole San Marzano tomatoes

One 14.5-ounce can whole San Marzano tomatoes

3 tablespoons olive oil

¼ pound pancetta, diced

1 medium onion, thinly sliced

4 cloves garlic, minced

1 teaspoon red pepper flakes

¼ cup chopped fresh basil

¼ cup chopped fresh parsley plus more, for garnish

½ cup freshly grated Pecorino Romano plus more, for garnish

Salt

Pepper

Cook fusilli per instructions on package until al dente.

Using your hands, crush the tomatoes into a medium mixing bowl, being sure to remove any hard cores as you go. Add any remaining liquid to the bowl.

In a large skillet over medium heat, heat the olive oil. Cook the pancetta until lightly browned, about 5 minutes. Remove to a plate.

In the same pan, cook the onions until soft, about 8 minutes. Add the garlic and red pepper flakes and cook another 2 minutes.

Add the basil and parsley and cook another 2 minutes.

Add the tomatoes and bring to a simmer. Cook for about 20 minutes, then add the cheese, salt, and pepper, adjusting the spices to your taste level.

Stir in the cooked fusilli and simmer until hot, about 5 minutes. Garnish with parsley and cheese and serve hot.

RAVIOLI GEORGE

PREP TIME: 10 MINUTES • COOK TIME: 50 MINUTES • YIELD: 6 TO 8 SERVINGS

As we were saying . . . just as a silly fusilli doll captures Jerry's personality, Kramer captures George's. How, you ask? With ravioli, naturally. Look, he inadvertently killed his fiancée and tried to poison his boss. GLC is no angel-hair pasta.

2 ¼ pounds spinach ravioli

2 tablespoons olive oil

2 medium onions, chopped

6 cloves garlic, chopped

6 cups fresh spinach, chopped

1½ cups cream, or milk

1½ cups shredded mozzarella, divided

1½ cups grated Parmesan, divided

1 teaspoon red pepper flakes

1 teaspoon salt

1 teaspoon pepper

1 teaspoon nutmeg

1 cup grape tomatoes, halved

Preheat the oven to 350°F.

Cook the ravioli according to the package instructions. Drain and set aside.

Heat the olive oil in a large Dutch oven over medium heat. Add the onions and cook until they start to brown, about 10 minutes. Add garlic and cook another 2 minutes. Add in the spinach and cook until wilted, about 3 minutes.

Add the cream and 1 cup of each of the cheeses. Add the red pepper flakes, salt, pepper, and nutmeg and cook until combined, about 3 minutes.

Add in the grape tomatoes and gently fold in the ravioli. Top with the remaining mozzarella and Parmesan cheeses.

Bake until the cheese is lightly browned, about 20 minutes, and serve hot.

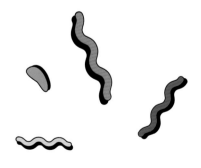

THE SEATTLE OF PESTO

PREP TIME: 5 MINUTES • YIELD: 2 CUPS

"Everybody's moving to Seattle." They are? If that's the case, then George has decided "it's the pesto of cities." And look, it's not like he has a track record of uninformed or deceitful comments, so it must be true. Likewise, this book is the pesto of *Seinfeld* cooking.

2 cups fresh basil leaves

2 tablespoons pine nuts

3 cloves garlic, peeled

½ cup best-quality extra-virgin olive oil

¾ cup grated Pecorino Romano cheese, or Parmesan cheese

1 teaspoon salt

½ teaspoon pepper

1 pound cooked pasta

Wash and dry the basil, removing the large stems.

In the bowl of a food processor, combine the basil and pine nuts and process for 1 minute. Add the garlic and process for 30 more seconds.

While the food processor is going, slowly pour the olive oil through the spout on the lid over the course of 1 minute.

Add the cheese, salt, and pepper and adjust to taste.

Serve with 1 pound of cooked pasta of your choice. If necessary, use a small amount of reserved pasta water to thin the pesto.

THE BUTTER SHAVE TURKEY

PREP TIME: 15 MINUTES • COOK TIME: 4 TO 5 HOURS PLUS 30 MINUTES RESTING TIME
YIELD: 8 TO 12 SERVINGS

"Stick a fork in me, Jerry. I'm done." The deliciousness of this bird and all of the trimmings will have you down for the count like Kramer. We advise not eating it on the roof in the hot sun and definitely NOT in the presence of Newman. He can't control himself.

½ cup (1 stick) unsalted butter, softened

1 cup grated Parmesan cheese

½ cup finely chopped mixed fresh herbs (like parsley, thyme, oregano, and rosemary)

4 cloves garlic, minced

1 teaspoon kosher salt

1 teaspoon pepper

One 18- to 20-pound whole turkey, cleaned and stuffed, if desired

Preheat the oven to 325°F.

Unwrap the turkey and remove the neck and giblets from the cavity. Rinse the bird inside and out, and pat dry.

In a medium mixing bowl, combine the butter, cheese, herbs, garlic, salt, and pepper.

Truss the turkey and place it in a roasting pan. Rub the butter mixture all over the turkey, including under the skin if desired.

Cover the turkey and roast for about 20 minutes per pound, if stuffed, and 15 minutes per pound, if not, until the temperature at the thickest part of the leg registers 165°F. Baste turkey with its juices occasionally while it's roasting and uncover the turkey for the final 20 to 30 minutes of cooking.

Remove from oven and let sit for 30 minutes before carving.

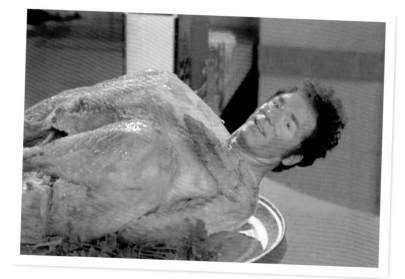

"FULLY SATISFYING"
PARMESAN RISOTTO

PREP TIME: 10 MINUTES • COOK TIME: 1 HOUR • YIELD: 6 SERVINGS

George's girlfriend Karen always feels full after the risotto. Contented? Satisfied? That's more than we can say for what George provides her. But after preparing this, anyone will feel robust. For true authenticity, have Babs Kramer there working at home as the bathroom attendant while you serve this dish to guests.

4 to 5 cups chicken or vegetable broth

2 tablespoons olive oil

1 medium yellow onion, minced

4 garlic cloves, minced

1 cup arborio rice

1 cup Parmesan cheese

Salt

Pepper

Fresh Italian parsley, chopped, for garnish

In a medium saucepan, warm the broth over medium heat. Simmer on low while you cook the risotto.

Heat the olive oil in a large skillet over medium-high heat, then add the onion. Cook, stirring often, until the onion starts to turn translucent, 6 to 8 minutes. Add the garlic and cook for another 2 minutes. Add the rice and cook for another 2 to 3 minutes to toast it.

Reduce heat to medium. Add about 1 cup of broth and stir the mixture until the liquid is fully absorbed, about 5 minutes. Repeat until you've added at least 4 cups of liquid. You'll know the risotto has enough liquid when it's no longer absorbing more and there is no crunch left to the rice grains when you test them. As you get closer to the end, add the liquid in smaller increments so you don't accidentally end up with watery risotto.

Remove the pan from the heat and stir in the Parmesan cheese. Season to taste with salt and pepper, and garnish with parsley.

Serve immediately as a side dish or top with grilled shrimp or chicken and serve as an entree.

KRAMER'S WON'T-KEEP CASSEROLE

PREP TIME: 15 MINUTES • COOK TIME: 30 MINUTES • YIELD: 6 SERVINGS

We'll supply the recipe, but the storage? You're on your own, Stringbean. The K-Man explains to Jerry that he whipped up one of these, but it "won't keep" due to a lack of proper Tupperware containers. We advise having yours on hand before tackling this one-stop meal.

1 pound egg noodles, cooked

Two 10.5-ounce cans condensed cream of mushroom soup

Two 5-ounce cans tuna packed in water, drained

1 cup frozen peas

One 4-ounce can sliced mushrooms

2 cups shredded cheddar cheese

½ teaspoon salt

2 tablespoons unsalted butter, melted

1 teaspoon garlic powder

1 teaspoon dried parsley

1 cup panko bread crumbs

Preheat the oven to 400°F.

In a large mixing bowl, combine the cooked noodles, mushroom soup, tuna, peas, mushrooms, cheddar cheese, and salt. Transfer to a large baking dish sprayed with nonstick cooking spray.

Bake for 20 minutes, then stir.

While the casserole is baking, combine the butter, garlic powder, parsley, and panko bread crumbs in a medium mixing bowl. After the casserole has baked for 20 minutes and you've stirred it, carefully spread the bread crumbs evenly over the top of the mixture.

Bake for another 10 minutes until topping is browned. Serve hot.

RUSTY'S BEEF-A-REENO

PREP TIME: 10 MINUTES • COOK TIME: 30 MINUTES • YIELD: 4 TO 6 SERVINGS

"Fit for a King and Queen-o" (and you!). Not just for horses, this dish captures the spirit of a cold New York evening, even if you're in the mood to, perhaps, attach a marble rye to a fishhook? Not that there's anything wrong with that. But when serving, remember: This meal isn't for a horse, and it's anyone's guess how the gastrointestinal workings of your guests are going to function.

2 cups macaroni

2 tablespoons neutral cooking oil

1 medium onion, chopped

3 cloves garlic, minced

1 pound ground beef

1 teaspoon salt

1 teaspoon pepper

1 tablespoon dried parsley

1 teaspoon paprika

One 14-ounce can tomato sauce

¼ cup tomato paste

1 cup freshly shredded cheddar cheese plus more, for garnish

In a large stockpot, cook the macaroni according to the package directions. Drain, reserving 2 cups of pasta water, and return the pasta to the stockpot.

Heat the oil in a large skillet over medium heat. Add the onion and cook until it starts to brown, about 10 minutes. Add the garlic and cook 2 more minutes.

Add the ground beef, salt, pepper, parsley, and paprika. Cook about 10 minutes, until ground beef is browned, then drain off any excess fat.

In a medium mixing bowl, combine the tomato sauce, tomato paste, and cheese. Add to the skillet and combine well with the meat mixture, cooking until hot.

Add the beef mixture to the pasta. Use pasta water, if necessary, to thin the sauce.

Serve garnished with more cheese.

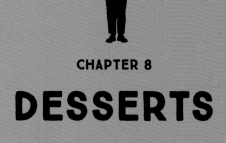

CHAPTER 8

DESSERTS

"Yours is a sweet tooth!" —Kramer
"THE SECRET CODE," SEASON 7

Though George may crave the salty snacks, the K-Man knows that his is "a sweet tooth!" Who among us can't resist a delectable dessert or something decadent, just like George Costanza himself? We can't blame him. Simply "look to the cookie" or sharpen that knife and fork to consume a Snickers bar—these ideas will NOT disappoint. A word of advice: If planning to use any butter-based frostings, don't leave them in a poorly ventilated basement for an extended period. . . . It may just put you through a historically rough punishment. Dismissed.

BLACK-AND-WHITE COOKIES

PREP TIME: 25 MINUTES • COOK TIME: 18 MINUTES • YIELD: 12 LARGE COOKIES

"Two races of flavor living side by side in harmony. . . . Look to the cookie, Elaine. Look to the cookie." Jerry is spot on. This two-toned party in your mouth is the ultimate, simple "*Seinfeld*ian" dessert. You don't even have to take a number to get one.

FOR THE COOKIES
½ cup (1 stick) salted butter

1 cup granulated sugar

1 large egg

2 teaspoons pure vanilla extract

¾ teaspoon baking powder

½ teaspoon baking soda

½ teaspoon salt

1½ cups all-purpose flour

⅓ cup buttermilk

FOR THE ICING
3 cups plus 2 tablespoons confectioners' sugar

4 tablespoons water

1 teaspoon pure vanilla extract

2 tablespoons unsweetened cocoa powder

TO MAKE THE COOKIES:

Preheat the oven to 350°F.

Line two baking sheets with parchment paper.

In the bowl of a mixer fitted with a flat beater, combine the butter and sugar. Beat on medium speed until the mixture is smooth, about 1 minute. Add the egg and vanilla and continue mixing 1 more minute. Add the baking powder, baking soda, and salt and mix with the mixer speed turned to low. Add half the flour and half the buttermilk, mix for 30 seconds, and repeat with the remaining flour and buttermilk, scraping down the sides of the bowl periodically.

Using a ¼ cup measuring cup, drop 6 evenly spaced cookies on each baking sheet, leaving at least 3 to 4 inches between them.

Bake for 15 to 18 minutes until cookies are just starting to brown.

Remove from the oven and slide the parchment paper off the baking sheets onto a heat-resistant surface to cool.

TO MAKE THE ICING:

In a medium mixing bowl, add the confectioners' sugar, water, and vanilla and whisk until all ingredients are combined. Separate out half of the mixture into a separate bowl and set aside.

Add 2 more tablespoons of confectioners' sugar and whisk until all sugar is incorporated. Transfer to a small bowl, cover with plastic wrap, and chill.

Return the second half of the icing mixture to the mixing bowl. Add cocoa powder and whisk until incorporated. Put the chocolate icing in a small bowl, cover it with plastic wrap, and chill it for 5 minutes before frosting the cookies.

Recipe continues on next page . . .

TO FROST THE COOKIES:

When cookies are completely cool and icing has chilled and set up, frost the cookies.

Cover half a cookie with a small piece of parchment paper to create a straight line down the center. Frost one side with the white icing and move to the next cookie. Once you have completed the white halves of all the cookies, go back and frost the other sides with chocolate icing.

When frosting has set up, cookies are ready to serve.

NO LESSER BABKA

PREP TIME: 45 MINUTES PLUS OVERNIGHT RISING TIME • COOK TIME: 35 MINUTES • YIELD: 2 LOAVES

"We can't show up at someone's house with Ring Dings and Pepsi!" Elaine has a point, much to George's chagrin, but if you follow her lead, this delightful babka won't disappoint. As Jerry says, "Cinnamon takes a backseat to no babka! . . . Cinnamon! Cinnamon! Again and again!" Just beware of stray hairs . . .

FOR THE DOUGH

4 cups all-purpose flour

½ cup granulated sugar

1 package instant yeast

1 teaspoon kosher salt

3 eggs

½ cup water plus 1 tablespoon

1 teaspoon pure vanilla extract

6 tablespoons unsalted butter, softened

1½ tablespoons neutral cooking oil

FOR THE CHOCOLATE FILLING

8 ounces dark chocolate chips

½ cup (1 stick) unsalted butter, softened

½ cup confectioners' sugar

¼ cup cocoa powder

⅛ teaspoon salt

FOR THE CINNAMON FILLING

½ cup (1 stick) unsalted butter, softened

1 cup granulated sugar

3 tablespoons ground cinnamon

TO MAKE THE DOUGH:

In the bowl of a mixer fitted with a dough hook, combine the flour, sugar, yeast, and salt and mix on medium-low speed. Add the eggs, water, and vanilla, and mix for another 2 minutes until the dough starts to form.

Add the butter and mix for another 10 minutes until the dough is smooth, pausing to scrape down the sides of the bowl.

Oil a medium mixing bowl, and while you have oil on your hands, transfer the dough into the bowl. Use the remaining oil to coat the dough. Cover tightly and let rise in the refrigerator overnight.

TO MAKE THE CHOCOLATE FILLING:

Place the chocolate chips in a medium mixing bowl and microwave for 60 seconds to melt. Stir until smooth.

Stir in the butter, then the sugar, cocoa powder, and salt. Mix, then set aside.

Recipe continues on page 135 . . .

TO MAKE THE CINNAMON FILLING:

In a medium mixing bowl, melt the butter by microwaving it for 30 seconds. Stir until smooth. Add the sugar and cinnamon and stir until combined. Set aside.

TO MAKE THE BABKA:

Remove the dough from the refrigerator, allow it to come to room temperature, and then divide it in half.

Preheat the oven to 350°F.

Spray two loaf pans with nonstick cooking spray.

On a floured surface, roll out half of the dough into a 14-by-10-inch rectangle and spread the chocolate filling over the top.

Starting with a long edge, roll the dough into a tight spiral, then slice the dough down the length of the roll so that you have two long halves. Braid the two halves into a helix pattern and place in a loaf pan.

Repeat steps 4 and 5 with the other half of the dough and the cinnamon filling.

Bake for 30 to 35 minutes until loaves are golden brown.

BEST APPLE PIE IN THE CITY

PREP TIME: 40 MINUTES • COOK TIME: 40 MINUTES • YIELD: 8 SERVINGS

There's only one correct answer when presented with a slice of this Monk's pie to eat: A resounding "Yes!" We'd accept a nonverbal "No" headshake for comedic effect, but ultimately, you won't do that, because you're not insane. EXACTLY. "Come on, try it!"

4 pounds assorted apples, peeled and cored

2 tablespoons unsalted butter

½ cup white sugar plus 1 tablespoon, divided

1½ teaspoons cinnamon

½ teaspoon nutmeg

½ teaspoon ground ginger

1 tablespoon cornstarch

1 tablespoon orange juice

2 pre-made pie dough discs

1 egg, beaten

Preheat the oven to 375°F.

Cut the apples into ¼-inch slices.

In a large sauté pan over medium heat, melt the butter. Add the apple slices, ½ cup of sugar, and the spices and sauté for 5 minutes, stirring occasionally, until apples start to soften. Sprinkle the cornstarch over the mixture and stir. Sauté another 5 minutes until apples start to soften.

Remove from the heat and allow to cool. Mix in the orange juice.

Lay one of the pie dough discs in a pie pan, making sure the dough lies flat to the bottom and sides. Pour in the fruit mixture, then lay the other pie dough on top, firmly crimping the edges together with your fingers or a fork. Cut vents into the top piece of dough. Brush the top with egg, then sprinkle with sugar.

Bake for 40 minutes or until crust is golden brown. Allow to cool before serving.

GEORGE'S "WHAT THE HELL? I'LL JUST EAT SOME TRASH" CHOCOLATE ÉCLAIR

PREP TIME: 1 HOUR, PLUS 2 HOURS TO OVERNIGHT CHILLING TIME
COOK TIME: 35 MINUTES • YIELD: 8 ÉCLAIRS

After one bite, YOU—not the éclair—will be hovering, like an angel. For true authenticity, and in a tribute to George, eat one over a trash receptacle. Though we'd advise keeping things neat and just using a plate.

FOR THE FILLING
2 cups whole milk

4 egg yolks

½ cup granulated sugar

3 tablespoons cornstarch

3 teaspoons pure vanilla powder

¼ cup (½ stick) unsalted butter, softened

FOR THE PASTRY
4 eggs

½ cup (1 stick) unsalted butter

1 cup water

1 teaspoon salt

1 tablespoon sugar

½ cup plus 2 tablespoons all-purpose flour

FOR THE CHOCOLATE GANACHE
½ cup heavy cream

¾ cup semisweet chocolate chips

TO MAKE THE FILLING:

In a medium saucepan, bring the milk to a simmer. Turn off the heat and allow to cool for 5 minutes.

In a medium bowl, whisk together the egg yolks and sugar. Add the cornstarch and vanilla and whisk until smooth. Slowly whisk in the warm milk.

Add the mixture back into the saucepan and cook over medium-high heat, whisking constantly to avoid curdling, until the custard has thickened and the mixture is at a gentle boil. Remove from the heat and whisk in the butter.

Return mixture to the mixing bowl and allow to cool slightly.

Cover the custard with plastic wrap, letting the wrap touch the top of the mixture to avoid a skin forming, and refrigerate for at least 2 hours or overnight.

TO MAKE THE PASTRY:

Preheat the oven to 425°F.

Line a baking sheet with parchment paper.

In a medium mixing bowl, whisk the eggs until beaten. Set aside.

In a medium saucepan over medium heat, melt the butter. Add the water, salt, and sugar and whisk until smooth. Add ½ cup of flour and whisk vigorously until there are no lumps in the mixture. Continue to heat the mixture for another 1 to 2 minutes, until the dough starts to stick to the bottom of the pan, so as to remove as much moisture as possible.

Remove the dough to the bowl of a mixer fitted with a flat beater. Mix on medium-low speed in 30-second intervals until it is no longer releasing any steam. The dough at this point should be room temperature to the touch.

While the mixer is running, add the egg mixture, a small amount at a time. When you've added about three-quarters of the egg mixture, test the dough. Turn off the mixer and raise the beater from the bowl—if the dough sticks to the beater, add more egg and test again. You will likely not use all of the mixture.

Transfer the dough into a large pastry bag fitted with a ⅞-inch-diameter round tip. Pipe out eight 5-inch-long éclairs onto the parchment-lined baking sheet, holding the pastry bag parallel to the sheet to get the most height possible out of the shape.

Bake at 425°F for 15 minutes, then reduce oven temperature to 375°F and bake for another 20 minutes, until pastries are just starting to turn golden brown.

Remove from the oven and immediately slide the parchment paper off the baking sheet onto a surface to cool.

When the pastry comes out of the oven, remove the custard from the refrigerator.

TO MAKE THE CHOCOLATE GANACHE AND ASSEMBLE THE ÉCLAIRS:

In a small saucepan over medium heat, warm the cream until it's bubbling around the edges. Remove from the heat and whisk in the chocolate chips, stirring constantly until smooth. Set aside.

When pastries are completely cooled, slice open one long edge of each éclair.

Transfer custard to a pastry bag fitted with a ½-inch round tip. Fill each pastry with custard, then close and spoon the ganache over the top.

You can prepare all the parts a day in advance, but don't assemble the éclairs until just before serving.

MR. PITT'S KNIFE AND FORK SNICKERS CAKE

PREP TIME: 45 MINUTES PLUS ABOUT ½ HOUR CHILLING TIME
COOK TIME: 50 MINUTES • YIELD: 12 SERVINGS

Some treats call for a little class. "How do you eat it? With your hands?" Channel Mr. Pitt and pay tribute to George as he lectures his colleagues and consumes his Snickers bar in the most erudite of styles: with a knife and fork, of course. If possible, the proper method includes watching PBS while eating, not Channel 11, because this could be the only chance to reach a stratosphere of society "that doesn't watch Channel 11!"

FOR THE CAKE

3 cups all-purpose flour

3 cups granulated sugar

1½ cup cocoa powder

2 teaspoons baking soda

2 teaspoons baking powder

1½ teaspoon salt

6 eggs

1½ cups buttermilk

½ cup vegetable oil

2 teaspoons vanilla extract

1 Snickers bar, thinly sliced, for decoration

FOR THE CARAMEL-PEANUT SAUCE

1 cup granulated sugar

½ cup water

½ cup heavy cream

Pinch of salt

½ cup lightly salted peanuts

FOR THE NOUGAT FILLING

½ cup (1 stick) salted butter, softened

¾ cup creamy peanut butter

½ cup Marshmallow Fluff

2 cups confectioners' sugar

1 teaspoon vanilla

3 tablespoons heavy cream

½ teaspoon powdered gelatin, or agar-agar

TO MAKE THE CAKE:

Preheat the oven to 350°F.

In a medium mixing bowl, combine the flour, sugar, cocoa powder, baking soda, baking powder, and salt.

In the bowl of a stand mixer, combine the eggs, buttermilk, oil, and vanilla and mix on low to combine. Slowly add the dry mix to the liquids and beat on medium until smooth. Remove bowl from the mixer and tap it on the counter to remove some of the air bubbles.

Spray three 8-inch round cake pans with nonstick cooking spray. Divide the batter evenly among the pans. You should have about 8 cups of batter total, so use about 2 ⅔ cups per pan.

Bake about 30 to 32 minutes, until a knife inserted in the center of the cake comes out with just a few crumbs. Remove from the oven and turn out onto a wire rack to cool.

Trim the tops of the cakes so they're flat and uniform in size.

TO MAKE THE CARAMEL-PEANUT SAUCE:

In a small saucepan over medium heat, heat the sugar and water together until the sugar is dissolved. Boil about 10 minutes until the mixture turns deep golden brown. (There is a very fine line between deep golden and burned—as soon as the mixture turns medium brown, remove it from the heat. If it looks or tastes burned, start over. It may take you a few attempts to get this right, but it's worth the effort.)

Off the heat, whisk in the cream slowly to avoid curdling the mixture and stir in the salt. Then stir in the peanuts and allow to cool completely.

Recipe continues on next page . . .

FOR THE CHOCOLATE GANACHE

½ cup heavy cream

¾ cup semisweet chocolate chips

TO MAKE THE NOUGAT FILLING:

In the bowl of a stand mixer fitted with a wire whip, beat the butter, peanut butter, and Marshmallow Fluff until combined. Add the sugar and vanilla and beat 1 minute until combined. While the mixer is operating, slowly pour in the cream and add the gelatin. Beat for 1 more minute.

Fill a piping bag fitted with a ⅜-inch round tip with nougat. Starting one-quarter inch in from the edge of the cake rounds, pipe a thick layer of nougat in a spiral pattern on the cut sides of two of the cake rounds. Reserve a small amount of nougat for decoration, but use most of it for these spirals.

Chill the cake layers in the refrigerator until ready to assemble.

TO MAKE THE CHOCOLATE GANACHE:

In a small saucepan over medium heat, heat the cream until very warm but not boiling. Remove from the heat and whisk in the chocolate chips until smooth. Set aside to cool.

TO ASSEMBLE THE CAKE:

Remove the two cake layers with nougat from the refrigerator.

Drop the cooled caramel-peanut sauce by the spoonful on top of the nougat filling and spread very carefully to make an even layer. You want the two layers to be distinct.

Place one layer on a serving plate, then top with the second layer, leaving the bare side of the top layer touching the frosted side of the bottom layer. Top with the third cake round.

If the ganache has been sitting long enough to congeal, warm it in a microwave oven for 10 seconds to allow it to drip properly. Slowly pour the ganache over the top of the cake, allowing the chocolate to pool on top and drip down over the sides.

Decorate the top of the cake with the last of the nougat and the slices of Snickers bar.

Chill until ready to serve.

SWEET SECRET BOSCO BROWNIES

PREP TIME: 10 MINUTES • COOK TIME: 35 MINUTES PLUS 10 TO 15 MINUTES COOLING TIME
YIELD: 24 BROWNIES

"Shout out your code, man!" How about a recipe instead? No secret password is required to unlock the deliciousness of these brownies. And honestly, we could've called these "Jor-El Brownies," but George's secret ATM code—not Jerry's—inspires this recipe. If, like George, yours is a sweet tooth, you won't be able to resist! Embarrassed by how many you might eat? Find an empty ATM vestibule for true authenticity and ambiance.

1 cup (2 sticks) unsalted butter, at room temperature

2 cups granulated sugar

2 tablespoons vanilla extract

3 large eggs

1 cup chocolate syrup (like Bosco)

½ cup cocoa powder

1 cup all-purpose flour

½ teaspoon salt

Preheat the oven to 350°F.

Spray a 9-by-13-inch baking pan with nonstick cooking spray.

In a large mixing bowl, whisk the butter and sugar. Add the vanilla and eggs and stir to combine. Stir in the chocolate syrup, then the cocoa powder, flour and salt.

Bake until a knife inserted into the center of the pan comes out not quite clean but not wet with batter, about 35 minutes.

Remove from the oven and allow to cool for 10 to 15 minutes. Cut into squares and serve.

MILKSHAKE FROM ABOVE

PREP TIME: 5 MINUTES • YIELD: 2 SERVINGS

"It's chocolate. It's peppermint. . . . It's very refreshing!" Grab a spot in the operating room and get to work with surgical precision to seal in the flavor. We suggest donning scrubs while you make this. One word of Cosmo Kramer–inspired advice: Don't use a retractor.

3 cups chocolate ice cream

1 cup milk

½ teaspoon peppermint extract

¼ cup Junior Mints plus more, for garnish

Whipped cream, for garnish

In a blender, combine the ice cream, milk, peppermint extract, and Junior Mints. Blend on high until smooth.

Divide into two glasses, garnish with additional mints and whipped cream, and serve.

CONCLUSION

Much like an incredulous Judge Art Vandelay rhetorically inquires during 'The Finale', we certainly "do not know how or under what circumstances" you found this book; but, in Jerry's words, "Let's cut the bull, sister"—you did and that's what matters.

For decades, *Seinfeld* fans have delighted in sharing the same inside jokes and references which instantly bring a smile, a knowing sustained laugh. That connection has helped the series to continue to entertain so many legions of fans even long after the show ceased producing new episodes. The impact is seen and felt immensely across the entire pop culture landscape, and this reach obviously includes food. You can't have a day filled with nothing and pondering life's inane and seemingly absurd trials and tribulations on an empty stomach.

We hope that the inspiration provided to us by the many unique characters who inhabit the *Seinfeld* universe has resulted in an enjoyable journey for all of you here within these pages. We can't see you, so we trust that after all of the inspiration and cooking surrounding the aforementioned recipes, you would, in the words of George "have a very-contented air." So, keep cooking, and plan some dishes for your next party: just don't invite be careful if you invite Joe Davola. Don't say we didn't warn you . . .

GLOSSARY

COOKING TERMS

BASTE: When a recipe calls for basting, it means to pour, soon, or brush liquid over food, most often meat or poultry, to give it good flavor and color during roasting.

CRIMP: To seal together the edges of two pieces of pastry dough by pressing the dough with the tines of a kitchen fork, the side of a knife, or a pastry crimper. Crimping is a good way to seal together securely the uncooked crusts of a double-crust pie, which may then be fluted if desired.

DREDGE: To coat with flour or another dry ingredient, such as cornmeal or bread crumbs, often seasoned. Food is sprinkled with the dry ingredient, dragged through it, or shaken with it. Alternatively, the food and coating may be placed in a plastic bag and shaken together. After dredging, the food should be shaken to remove excess coating. Do not dredge food too far in advance of cooking, or the coating will absorb moisture from the food and become gummy. Laying dredged food on a wire tack also helps avoid gumminess. Dredging food is usually sauteed, fried or deep-fried, or baked. The coating helps it brown nicely and retain moisture, and adds a nice crispiness.

JULIENNE: Refers to cutting food into long, thin strips, which in turn are called a "julienne."

KNEAD: Uncover the dough and knead it by using the heel of one hand to push the dough away from you and then pull it back with your fingertips. Turn and repeat until the dough is smooth and elastic, 5–7 minutes.

MINCE: Gather the leaves together and rock the blade over them until they are chopped into small, even pieces (finely chopped), or into pieces as fine as possible (minced).

REDUCE: Simmering or boiling a liquid, such as broth or wine, is a good way to enhance flavor. As you do so, the quantity of the liquid decreases, and the liquid thickens into a flavorful sauce.

RISE: Traditionally, bread dough rises two times, but sometimes you have to change your habits and ignore logic. Sometimes, as with overnight rolls, I have a very long first rise followed by a shorter rising after shaping. Some of the sourdough breads rest for only a short while before shaping and then rise much longer in the second stage instead. The important point is that the dough is well risen when it's time to bake it. You can always slow down the rising by keeping the dough cool. It is difficult to recommend exact timings but, for example, dough that I let rise for two hours at room temperature might take twice as long when refrigerated. You have to experiment. Another aspect of rising to keep in mind is that a firm dough usually rises more slowly than a moist dough.

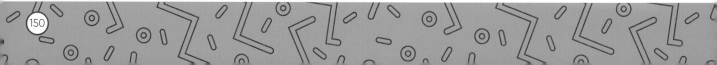

ROAST: Roasting meats and poultry in an uncovered roasting pan in a hot oven intensifies their flavors. Because the oven does most of the work, this technique requires little hands-on cooking time. Before you start, line a heavy roasting pan with aluminum foil and brush the foil with a little olive oil to help prevent sticking.

SAUTÉ: Taken from the verb "to jump" in French, sauté means to cook quickly in a small amount of fat. The pan should be preheated with the fat before adding foods so that they sear quickly, and there should be plenty of room in the pan so that foods don't get crowded and simmer in their own juices.

SIMMER: Simmering calls for consistent, medium-to-small bubbles . . .Simmering and poaching are moist-heat cooking techniques that gently cook foods to tenderness in a hot liquid . . .You don't need special cookware for simmering. Any saucepan or sauté pan will do, although if you intend to reduce a volume of liquid, a pan with a wide base and large surface area will help the process go faster.

STEAM: Steaming is a gentle cooking method that retains the food's shape, color, flavor, and texture . . .During cooking, the rising steam released from a boiling liquid surrounds the food to cook it gently . . .Steaming involves gently cooking food while suspended over boiling water in a tightly covered pot.

TRUSS: Trussing, or tying, a whole turkey yields a plump roast bird with a tidy shape, making it easier to carve. This technique can also be used for whole roasted chickens and Cornish game hens. (However, keep in mind that trussing can cause areas such as the inner thigh joint to receive uneven heat and be underdone when the rest of the bird is ready. Turning the bird in the oven can combat uneven cooking.) When you truss, use sturdy, linen kitchen string, which is less likely than cotton to scorch. Once the bird is done, snip the string off before carving and serving the turkey.

INGREDIENTS

ACTIVE DRY YEAST: Available in ¼oz (7g) packages containing 2¼ teaspoons yeast. Be sure to check the date on the package to make sure the yeast is truly active. Contrary to what the package says, you don't have to use warm water.

AGAR-AGAR: Agar-agar is sold in long strands or sticks. It may be soaked and eaten in soups like noodles, but its primary use throughout East Asia is as a gelatin-like thickener. In the West, agar-agar is prized by vegetarians as a replacement for animal-based gelatin.

CAKE FLOUR: Milled from soft wheat and containing cornstarch, cake flour is low in protein and high in starch. It gives cakes a light crumb. Cake flour has also undergone a bleaching process that increases its ability to hold water and sugar, so cakes made with cake flour are less likely to fall.

GANACHE: When freshly made, this smooth mixture of chocolate, cream, and butter is a thick, pourable sauce that makes a delicious accompaniment to cake slices. When cooled and set, ganache can be used as an icing for cakes and cookies.

INSTANT YEAST: A third kind of active dry yeast, instant dried yeast, is three times more powerful than active dry yeast. Also called European yeast, it is a stronger, more stable yeast developed for commercial bakers. Some bakers feel that it has an objectionable taste, and it should not be used in sweet bread doughs or those that require long, slow risings.

ROUX: A roux is a combination of fat, usually butter, and flour used for thickening sauces and soups. Different recipes call for different proportions of ingredients. In a heavy-bottomed pan over medium heat, melt the butter or heat the oil. Then, whisk in the flour until smooth.

TAHINI PASTE: This paste, made from ground sesame seeds, has a rich, creamy flavor and a concentrated sesame taste. Tahini, also called sesame paste, is used in the popular chickpea spread known as hummus and in baba ghanoush, a Middle Eastern eggplant puree. It is also combined with lemon juice and seasonings to make taratoor, a thin Middle Eastern sauce used as a dip for vegetables and pita bread, as a dressing for salads, and as a sauce for fish, vegetables, and falafel. The oil often separates from the paste and should be stirred in before using.

COOKING UTENSILS

BAKING DISH: Shallow, rectangular dishes made of tempered glass, porcelain, or earthenware are all-purpose vessels that work for roasting meat or vegetables and baking brownies or bread pudding. Items will cook more slowly in opaque ceramic than they will in clear glass.

BAKING PAN: Use these pans, which typically measure 13 by 9 inches with sides 2 to 2½ inches high, for baking sheet cakes, brownies, corn bread and coffee cakes. You can also use these pans for making casseroles.

BAKING SHEET: A baking sheet (also called a sheet pan) is a rectangular metal pan with shallow, slightly sloping rims. Choose sturdy stainless-steel ones that will last for years.

CAKE PAN: Round pans, generally 2 inches deep and 8 or 9 inches in diameter, used especially for baking cakes. You will want to have at least two on hand for making layer cakes.

DOUGH HOOK: Most of the various types of dough hooks that I've tested managed to knead the dough well. Some mixers have a dough hook that moves in an attached bowl; others have a bowl that revolves on a small platter. The size of the bowl is even more important, I think. Surprisingly, many stand mixers come with a bowl that is too small, so if you are going to bake large amounts, carefully check the details when purchasing a stand mixer.

DUTCH OVEN: A large heavy cooking pot usually made of cast iron. This can go on the stove or in the oven and is great at retaining heat, making it the perfect cooking vessel for just about everything.

FOOD PROCESSOR: An electronic kitchen tool that consists of a plastic bowl fitted over a set of spinning blades, which can be used to assist in a variety of food prep, including chopping, shredding, pulverizing, mixing, and more. Usually comes with at least two speeds and a pulse option to create short bursts of processing. More commonly (but not exclusively) used to prep dry ingredients before cooking.

IMMERSION BLENDER: Also called hand or handheld blenders, immersion blenders have an extended blade that is immersed in a food or mixture to blend of puree it. Immersion blenders are great for pureeing food in the container in which it is mixed or cooked. This means that they can blend larger amounts of food than will fit in the jar of a standing blender. Immersion blenders also tend to incorporate more air into a liquid and as such can be used to make a frothy foam on creamed soups. These blenders usually have only two speeds, and the blade must be completely immersed in the food to prevent spattering. Many are designed to hang in a wall mount for easy storage. Some have whisk attachments or small containers for blender smaller amounts of food.

MEAT THERMOMETER: Every kitchen should have a meat thermometer. There are two kinds: a probe type, which is inserted into the meat at the beginning of cooking and left there until the proper temperature is reached, and an instant-read type, which is inserted toward the end of the cooking period to test for doneness . . .Insert a meat thermometer in the center of a piece of meat or a roast, or on the inside of the thickest part of the thigh of a bird; make sure the thermometer is not touching bone.

MIXER: Two basic types of motor-driven electric mixers are available, stand or standing and handheld or portable, and each has its place in the kitchen. Stand mixers are stationary machines good for large amounts and heavy batters.

PARING KNIFE: A small, evenly proportioned blade usually 3 to 4 inches long. Used for paring, peeling, and slicing fruits and vegetables and for chopping small quantities.

PASTRY BAG: A pastry bag is a cone-shaped bag which is usually used to pipe frosting or icing on cakes, cookies, cupcakes, and other desserts. These come in disposable and reusable options and usually come with a set of attachable tips to create different shapes in your frosting. Some disposable options are microwave-safe, which is useful for melting chocolate or other items (be sure to check the packaging before trying this). Aside from decorating desserts, they can also be used to pipe batter, dough, creams, or pureed ingredients ahead of cooking.

SAUCEPAN: This simple round pan has either straight or slightly sloping sides and generally ranges in size from 1 to 5 quarts. If you are buying only one, consider a 2-quart saucepan, which is most versatile. The pans are designed to facilitate rapid evaporation so that a sauce thickens and cooks efficiently. Straight-sided pans with high sides are ideal for longer cooking, since the liquid will not evaporate as quickly.

SAUTÉ PAN: Sauté pans have high, angled handles and relatively high sides to help prevent food from bouncing out of the pan when it is being stirred, turned, or flipped. The sides can range from 2½ to 4 inches high, with 3 inches being the most popular. Sauté pans can measure from 6 to 14¼ inches in diameter, and volume capacities generally range from 1 to 7 quarts, with 2½ to 4 quarts being the most useful for home cooks. Sauté pans often come with lids, which are useful for containing evaporation in recipes that call for long, gentle simmering. For this reason, sauté pans are also nicely suited to braises or any stove top recipes that call for large amounts of liquid.

SKILLET: Also called a frying pan, this broad pan is often confused with a sauté pan, but traditionally differs in that it has sides that flare outward, making it useful for cooking foods that must be stirred or turned out of the pan. Most kitchens should have both a smaller one, 9 or 10 inches across the bottom, and a larger one, 12 or 14 inches. Skillets do not have lids. The best materials are anodized aluminum or cast iron; if you buy two, make one of them nonstick.

WOK: This versatile Chinese pan is ideal for stir-frying, deep-frying, and steaming. Traditionally made of plain carbon steel, the wok has a rounded bottom that allows small pieces of food to be rapidly tossed and stirred. It also has high, gradually sloping sides to help keep food circulating inside the pan during stir-frying. In Western kitchens, round-bottomed woks are held in place over gas burners by a metal ring that allows the flames to rise and distribute heat around the pan. Woks with flat bottoms have also been developed to sit securely and distribute heat more efficiently on electric burners. Woks can have one long and one short handle, or two short handles, depending on the manufacturer. They are sometimes sold with a lid for steaming.

KITCHEN MEASUREMENTS

CUP	TBSP	TSP	FL OZ
⅟₁₆ cup	1 tbsp	3 tsp	½ fl oz
⅛ cup	2 tbsp	6 tsp	1 fl oz
¼ cup	4 tbsp	12 tsp	2 fl oz
⅓ cup	5⅓ tbsp	16 tsp	2⅔ fl oz
½ cup	8 tbsp	24 tsp	4 fl oz
⅔ cup	10⅔ tbsp	32 tsp	5⅓ fl oz
¾ cup	12 tbsp	36 tsp	6 fl oz
1 cup	16 tbsp	48 tsp	8 fl oz

CELSIUS	FAHRENHEIT
93°C	200°F
107°C	225°F
121°C	250°F
135°C	275°F
149°C	300°F
163°C	325°F
177°C	350°F
191°C	375°F
204°C	400°F
218°C	425°F
232°C	450°F

GALLON	QUART	PINT	CUP	FL OZ
⅟₁₆ gal	¼ qt	½ pints	1 cup	8 fl oz
⅛ gal	½ qt	1 pints	2 cup	16 fl oz
¼ gal	1 qt	2 pints	4 cup	32 fl oz
½ gal	2 qt	4 pints	8 cup	64 fl oz
1 gal	4 qt	8 pints	16 cup	128 fl oz

DIETARY CONSIDERATIONS

	VEGETARIAN	VEGAN	GLUTEN-FREE
BREAKFASTS			
Mr. Lippman's Elaine's Muffin Tops	✓		
Jerry's Cereal Bars	✓		
Newman's Coffee Cake	✓		
Forbidden Bagels		✓	
"Certain Time" Cantaloupe Breakfast Bowl	✓		
Kramer's Peach Pancakes	✓		
NO DOUBLE-DIPPING			
Hummus Among Us		✓	✓
Onion Dip	✓		✓
Baked Queso Dip	✓		✓
Hot Spinach Artichoke Dip	✓		
#1 Salsa in America		✓	✓
Mrs. Choate's Marble Rye		✓	
A LITTLE NOSH			
Puffy Shirt Pastry Tarts	✓		
George's Jerk Store Shrimp			✓
Kramer's Peterman Reality Tour Pizza Bagels	✓		
Jerry's "Dates"			✓
These Pretzels Will Make You Thirsty	✓		
Hand Model Hand Pies			
NO SOUP FOR YOU			
Newman's Jambalaya			✓
Elaine's Mulligatawny Soup		✓	✓
George's Turkey Chili			✓
Yev's Black Bean Soup	✓		✓
Yev's Mushroom Barley Soup		✓	✓
Yev's Chicken Broccoli Soup			✓
Yada Yada Yada Lobster Bisque			

	VEGETARIAN	VEGAN	GLUTEN-FREE

MONK'S CAFE

	VEGETARIAN	VEGAN	GLUTEN-FREE
George's Bedroom Pastrami			
Jerry's Vegetable Sandwich	✓		
Jerry's Egg White Omelet			✓
Elaine's Big Salad			✓
George's Usual: Tuna on Toast			
The Opposite of Tuna on Toast			

TAKEOUT

	VEGETARIAN	VEGAN	GLUTEN-FREE
Kramer Wants a Papaya King Hot Dog			
Steinbrenner Special Calzone			
Across the Street Supreme Flounder			✓
Elaine's Submarine Captain Sub			
Kenny's Roaster Chicken			
Puddy's Favorite Sandwich			
Long Wait Lo Mein	✓		

DINNER

	VEGETARIAN	VEGAN	GLUTEN-FREE
Festivus Meatloaf			
Jerry's "Just a Salad"		✓	✓
Franco's Chops			
Cosmo's Unseen Bouillabaisse			✓
Man-Hands Lobster			✓
Make Your Own Pizza Pie			
Fusilli Jerry			
Ravioli George	✓		
The Seattle of Pesto	✓		
The Butter Shave Turkey			✓
"Fully Satisfying" Parmesan Risotto	✓		✓
Kramer's Won't-Keep Casserole			
Rusty's Beef-A-Reeno			

DESSERTS

	VEGETARIAN	VEGAN	GLUTEN-FREE
Black and White Cookies	✓		
No Lesser Babka	✓		
Best Apple Pie in the City	✓		
George's "What the Hell? I'll Just Eat Some Trash" Chocolate Éclair	✓		
Mr. Pitt's Knife and Fork Snickers Cake	✓		
Sweet Secret Bosco Brownies	✓		
Milkshake from Above	✓		✓

ABOUT THE AUTHORS

JULIE TREMAINE is a food and travel writer whose work has appeared in outlets such as Forbes, Bloomberg Next, Yahoo!, Yankee Magazine, and Providence Monthly, where she was executive editor and creative director. Read more of her writing at Travel-Sip-Repeat.com.

A self-proclaimed "Master of the *Seinfeld* domain," **BRENDAN KIRBY** has been obsessed with "Nothing" since he first saw the show in eighth grade. Helping to greatly inspire his love of comedy and joke writing, the show was a focal point of his formative years—the result of having absolutely no life whatsoever in high school; eerily similar to his life today. He makes his home in Rhode Island, and you can catch him weekdays at 9am on the CBS affiliate in Providence as cohost of the daily, live entertainment talk program, *The Rhode Show*—a career that enables him to do three of his favorite things: make jokes on TV, wear makeup, and write his own fan mail under the name Bob Sacamano. You can follow him on social media @BrendanKirbyTV.

INSIGHT
EDITIONS

PO Box 3088
San Rafael, CA 94912
www.insighteditions.com

Find us on Facebook: www.facebook.com/InsightEditions
Follow us on Twitter: @insighteditions

ISBN: 978-1-64722-764-7

PUBLISHER: RAOUL GOFF
VP OF LICENSING AND PARTNERSHIPS: VANESSA LOPEZ
VP OF CREATIVE: CHRISSY KWASNIK
VP OF MANUFACTURING: ALIX NICHOLAEFF
VP, EDITORIAL DIRECTOR: VICKI JAEGER
DESIGNER: MEGAN SINAED-HARRIS
SENIOR EDITOR: JUSTIN EISINGER
EDITOR: ANNA WOSTENBERG
EDITORIAL ASSISTANT: SAMANTHA ALVARADO
MANAGING EDITOR: MARIA SPANO
PRODUCTION ASSOCIATE: DEENA HASHEM
SR PRODUCTION MANAGER, SUBSIDIARY RIGHTS: LINA S PALMA-TENEMA

BIG THANKS TO THE NEW YORK PHOTO TEAM:
PHOTOGRAPHER: EMILY HAWKES
PHOTO ASSISTANT: REGINA TAMBURRO
FOOD STYLIST: ERIKA JOYCE
FOOD STYLING ASSISTANT: AARON MEFTAH
PROPS STYLIST: ANDREA GRECO
PROP STYLING ASSISTANTS: TODD HENRY & JILL SEYMOUR
PA: ANDREW LEWIS

Images on pages 32 and 136 from Shutterstock

REPLANTED PAPER   ROOTS of PEACE

Insight Editions, in association with Roots of Peace, will plant two trees for each tree used
in the manufacturing of this book. Roots of Peace is an internationally renowned humanitarian
organization dedicated to eradicating land mines worldwide and converting war-torn lands into
productive farms and wildlife habitats. Roots of Peace will plant two million fruit and nut trees in
Afghanistan and provide farmers there with the skills and support necessary for sustainable land use.

Manufactured in China by Insight Editions
10 9 8 7 6 5 4 3 2 1